# VITAL
# integrities

# V I T A L
# integrities

## how values-based leaders acquire
## and preserve their credibility

# GEORGE BRYMER

ALL
SQUARE

All Square, Inc., Toledo, Ohio
© 2005 by George A. Brymer, Jr.
All rights reserved. Published 2005
Printed in the United States of America
14 13 12 11 10 09 08 07 06 05          1 2 3 4 5

ISBN-13: 978-0-9766335-9-4
ISBN-10: 0-9766335-9-0

Publisher's Cataloging-in-Publication *(Provided by Quality Books, Inc.)*

Brymer, George.
    Vital integrities : how values-based leaders acquire
and preserve their credibility / George Brymer.
    p. cm.
    Includes bibliographical references and index.
    LCCN 2005901811
    ISBN-13: 978-0-9766335-9-4
    ISBN-10: 0-9766335-9-0

    1. Leadership.    I. Title.

HD57.7.B796 2005          658.4'092
                     QBI05-600002

This book is printed on 50 percent postconsumer recycled paper,
processed chlorine free.

*For Vicky*

# Contents

# Acknowledgements

I always knew that writing a book would consume a lot of my time. But I never expected that it would be such a burden on my friends. I wish to acknowledge some of my favorite people for their assistance, suggestions, constructive criticism, and emotional support during this project.

Thanks to my proofreading friends, Dr. Cynthia Beekley, Bil Homka, and Ryan Hacker, for their willingness to read the raw manuscript. They spent countless hours pouring over the first drafts, and provided honest, invaluable feedback on the content. Thanks to Cynthia for her bluntness ("What do you mean by this?") that forced me to add clarity. Thanks to Bil for his thoughtful—and humorous—margin queries. And thanks to Ryan for both his keen eyes and his constant encouragement. Since I can't give them back the time they sacrificed on this effort, I hope they'll accept my grateful acknowledgement of their contributions to this book.

Thanks to my new friend, Laurel Marshfield. I sought out an editor who could find spelling, punctuation, and grammar mistakes in my manuscript. Luckily for me—and for you the reader—I found Laurel, because she provided so much more. She showed me how to improve my writing without altering the message I wanted to convey. She somehow sensed when I had left assumptions behind in my head, and showed me how to get those thoughts into the book. Best of all, she expressed interest in my success as an author. I owe her a special word of gratitude.

Thanks also to my creative friend, Rob Davis, for designing a cover that is as memorable as it is distinctive. One of Rob's gifts as a designer is the ability to communicate a concept like leadership through a universal, visual language. I truly appreciate his contribution to this project.

Since I drew the ideas for this book from my real-life leadership experiences, I'm also grateful to the many friends who were once my co-workers—everyone who ever reported to me, and everyone to whom I ever reported. All of my bosses taught me something about leadership—even when, through their behavior, it was what *not* to do. Likewise, I learned something from everyone I ever led. Without a doubt, some employees had to endure my on-the-job training and, for that, I offer my sincere apology. I shall always be indebted to my current and former colleagues for inspiring me to become a better leader.

Foremost, thanks to my *best* friend, my wife Vicky, for her love and unconditional support in everything I do. Everyone who knows us, knows us as a team. She has read this book more than anyone else ever will. But while others helped make this book what it is, she helps make me who I am. Her inspiration is behind everything I have ever accomplished. I have dedicated this book—as I have my life—to her.

George Brymer

# V I T A L
# integrities

# Preface

*Wonder: Verb. To be affected with surprise,
curiosity, or doubt; to wait with uncertain
expectation; to question or speculate.*

All truly passionate business leaders are works in progress, constantly striving to improve their effectiveness, and looking for ways to sustain their professional existence. I wrote this book to help leaders move forward in their leadership progression. My intent is to help managers at all levels improve, to help them expand their leadership skills, and to help them find greater enjoyment in their roles as leaders.

I believe that integrity is what leadership is all about. I've spent nearly three decades in leadership positions, including a nineteen-year engagement with a *Fortune* 500 bank. I've presided over technology workers and fry cooks, clerical staffs and salespeople, ambitious up-and-comers and working stiffs, highly paid professionals and nonprofit volunteers. I keep returning to the same conclusion: people are searching for leaders with integrity who prove their credibility continuously.

But how do you prove your credibility? To help current and future leaders answer that question, I created *The Leading from the Heart Workshop*®, a three-day program devoted to teaching values-based leadership. The workshop is a vehicle for sharing my experiences, research, ideas, and enthusiasm for the leadership craft. This book, like the workshop, focuses on six behaviors that

I determined are common to values-based leaders, practices I refer to as "Vital Integrities." Leaders who are values-based:

- Accept challenges and take risks
- Master both listening and speaking
- Live by the values they profess
- Freely give away their authority
- Recognize the best in others
- Have a vision and convince others to share it

This book contains detailed descriptions of the six Vital Integrities, along with illustrations explaining how they complement and interact with one another.

*Vital Integrities* relates leadership as I teach it in my workshops, so it may seem different from other management books. In fact, it *is* different. This book focuses more on awareness than on techniques. Experience has shown me that trying to teach a systemic approach to leadership—when this happens, do that—is a waste of time, because no single method can cover every situation that might arise. I have found that leaders learn faster, and retain the information longer, when they learn why and how at the same time.

A point of clarification: employing the Vital Integrities is not about changing your organization's values. Too many misguided enterprises, struggling with leadership challenges, hope to generate inspiration simply by rewriting their mission statements. Instead, Vital Integrities are leadership actions that, when practiced proactively, demonstrate your organization's existing values and further establish your credibility as a leader.

While exploring this practical, battle-tested approach to values-based leadership, new managers will discover essential survival skills, and experienced leaders will gain a fresh perspective on helping employees remain committed to their organizations. In fact, there's help in this book not only for managers, but also for supervisors, team leaders, and professionals at all levels. Whether you are just starting your leadership journey, or are an experienced pro looking to get back on course, the six Vital Integrities will serve as your guide.

This book's emphasis is on helping you lead others, but you will also find recommendations for applying values-based leadership skills to your other relationships, including with those to whom you report. Let's face it: the best leaders understand how to lead from all directions. And past participants in *The Leading from the Heart Workshop* have also reported success in applying the six Vital Integrities not only at work, but in their roles as spouses, parents, grandparents, sons and daughters, and friends. In fact, you will find the Vital Integrities helpful in any relationship that cherishes values.

One final thought before we start exploring the Vital Integrities. Our employees spend too much time *wondering*. Some question whether the job security they are depending on is certain. Some doubt whether a coveted raise or promotion is imminent. Employees may begin to wonder, if not worry, when confronted with a manager whose behavior flies in the face of the company mission statement. Employees can trust their leaders, remain loyal to their organizations, and do their jobs effectively only when their minds are free of wonder. Therefore, this book's ultimate goal is to help you put an end to your employees' needless wondering.

# Introduction

## Welcome to the Age of Corporate Governance

A national workplace study conducted in 2003 revealed that just 30 percent of U.S. workers are loyal to their employers—that is, they feel a personal connection, are apt to recommend their organizations to others, and are resistant to offers from outside employers.[1] In 2004, a human resources consulting firm found that only half of all U.S. workers, just 51 percent, trust their organization's senior leaders.[2] Diminishing trust and loyalty levels may in part reflect "fallout" from the many highly publicized corporate scandals of recent years, and how these disgraces have affected employees at all institutions.

We create stereotypes when we base opinions about an entire group on the behavior of a few members, and we seem to be doing that now with business leaders. Newspapers report daily on investigations into corruption involving companies like Enron, Arthur Anderson, Global Crossing, WorldCom, and Tyco. Business leaders face accusations of overstating earnings, hiding massive debt, diverting millions of dollars in company funds for their personal use, using questionable accounting practices, and obstructing justice. Is it any wonder many employees develop biases that lead them to associate their leaders with dishonesty and untrustworthiness?

Trust and employee loyalty are interdependent. When employees mistrust their leaders, or are ashamed of their organization's behavior, they are more likely to leave.[3] Employees feeling trapped—those who doubt they can find a job that pays the same, feel reliant on a specific benefit, or consider their skills inadequate—might stay, but their fading commitment is damaging to productivity. And crumbling confidence is harmful to the bottom line, whether you measure your bottom line in dollars earned or clients served.

Increasing mistrust and vanishing loyalty come at a challenging time for hiring and retaining employees. According to the U.S. Department of Labor's Bureau of Labor Statistics, employment between the years 2002 and 2012 will increase by 21 million jobs. But the Bureau projects that the civilian labor force will grow by only 17 million people in the same period. That's a shortfall of 4 million workers for the available jobs projected for 2012.[4]

Service industries will account for most of the decade's newly created jobs. Education and health services, as well as professional and business services will grow twice as fast as the overall economy.[5] And the workforce is aging. The number of workers age fifty-five or older will grow by half, a growth rate four times that of the general workforce, so that one out of five workers will be in that age group by 2012.[6]

An ongoing shift in what workers search for in their employers further muddles the hiring and retention process. In the late 1960s and early 1970s, baby boomers embraced the ideology of the day. Once they realized that principles are good but bills are persistent, the boomers went to work. And they worked hard, putting in long hours, chasing salaries that would allow them to improve on their parents' lot. However, now scores of boomers are trying to make up for "selling out" to corporate America. Although they enjoyed the financial rewards of their efforts, countless members of this generation also experienced the downside: they either lost jobs to layoffs, or know someone who did. Trying to salvage some self respect, boomers are now gravitating toward jobs that provide meaning.

Generation X, meanwhile, was the first generation of latchkey kids. Whereas the Industrial Revolution drew fathers outside the home to work, Gen Xers probably grew up in households in which both parents held jobs. Many learned to deal with life issues early, thanks to divorced parents or those living "permissive" lifestyles. Highly spiritual, Gen Xers are determined to resist their parents' example, by placing less emphasis on their own pleasure and more emphasis on doing good things for others. Generation X makes up the largest percentage of volunteers in the country, and this generation of workers is looking for employers who support those efforts.

Generation Y came next, the Internet Generation. Information rich, Netters also reaped the material benefits produced by their baby boomer parents' hard work and dual incomes. Many Netters enter the workforce with an air of entitlement and most exhibit a sense of immediacy. Don't bother explaining your organization's 401(k) plan; Gen Y job candidates want the money up front. But can we blame them? Having watched their parents' employers repay years of loyalty by their eliminating jobs, Gen Yers fully understand the employment-at-will concept. That's why workers from Generation Y scrutinize the values statements of potential employers, ignore long-term promises, and look for values that seem realistic.

When selecting employers, job candidates from all generations are focusing less on the financial rewards and more on the values rewards. Today, people seek out employers whose values are consistent with their own, and look for ways to satisfy their interests and needs by aligning with an organization's mission.

## In the war for talent, everyone is fighting over your best employees.

Fact is, in the face of waning loyalty and mounting suspicion, there is growing competition for employees. Furthermore, in the war for talent, your best employees are every other employer's brightest prospects. For many organizations, the new reality means reassessing their leadership approaches, flattening their hierarchies, and emphasizing their core values. And they must do all these things quickly, before their organizations become extinct.

## Values and Their Organizational Impact

To attract customers and workers, employers must be able to make their organizations stand out from the crowd. It takes more than just goods or services to create the strategic edge needed to market your wares or recruit top talent. Too many competitors make the products you manufacture, provide the services you offer, or meet the social needs you fill, as well. These days, customers "buy" the *people* making the merchandise or performing the services. Employees are more than just cogs in a machine; they are your organization's identity and its character, too. Increasingly, both customers and job candidates migrate toward the whole organization—its products, its people, its culture, and its values.

To convey their message to customers and employees alike, organizations create mission statements. Mission statements identify the organization's purpose, describe its philosophy, and establish a distinctive marketing position. Specifying core values in the mission statement helps inspire a culture and drive the employee behavior necessary to achieve the organization's goals, whether that constitutes making money, or serving a specific sector of society.

Mission statements typically include these often mentioned values:

- showing people dignity, respect, and courtesy
- providing the highest quality products, work, or customer service— *excellence in everything we do*
- maintaining morals, ethics, and trust—*the highest standards of conduct*
- community service
- employee appreciation and development—*people are our greatest asset*
- open communication
- accountability
- teamwork
- appreciating diversity, going beyond equal rights and equal opportunities
- religious faith
- protecting the environment—promoting conservation
- profit—*shareholder value*

How did mission statements originate? In the beginning, the board of directors went on a three-day retreat up to the mountains or into the woods. While there, those leaders created the organization's mission statement. Someone undoubtedly said, "Let's say something about people being our greatest asset." Another recommended, "Some of our employees need more training—let's add something about helping them develop." And so on. When they returned, the Board gave their mission statement to the marketing department to tweak the language, arrange the printing, and produce the poster that hangs in the lobby today.

A typical mission statement might describe an organization's values with language similar to the following:

> We firmly believe that our organization's greatest asset is its people. We encourage and provide for professional development activities that help achieve our goals. We take personal responsibility, are individually accountable, and follow core values that direct our daily actions.

Suppose you are a job candidate with a strong interest in getting ahead. You want an employer who will exploit your current abilities and make an investment in teaching you new skills. Also, you're passionate about accountability. After all, you've labored in companies that tolerated freeloaders and you plan to avoid doing that again. You stumble on a prospective employer with the mission statement above. This company declares its staff as its greatest asset. It supports professional development—heck, it encourages it! And it's accountable: "We take personal responsibility." At last, you've found an organization with values that match your own. You have discovered an organization to join.

Picture yourself there, working your way up the ladder. The company has sent you to some classes. Perhaps management assigned you a mentor. You're taking responsibility for your work and earning just compensation for your efforts. Sure, you observe some people doing just enough to get by; however, management deals with them fairly, and reserves raises and promotions for hard-working people like you. Now you can fix your attention on doing great work and helping your employer's business flourish. Everything is going according to plan.

Fast forward. After a few years at the company, as invariably happens, you begin reporting to a different manager. And it turns out your new supervisor is a cost containment fanatic. "No more squandering money on something as intangible as training," your boss announces. Your new leader also feels awkward discussing performance shortcomings with employees. Some coworkers are slacking, but this boss shrinks from the slightest confrontation. Your manager's behavior runs counter to the values that attracted you to the company in the first place. Suddenly, you are out of alignment with your organization.

The organization's values have probably remained unchanged, but your leader's actions cause you to wonder. You question if this is the place for you, after all. When asked why you are leaving, you say, "Because this place has changed." But, in reality, you are leaving your manager.

After you go, senior management will inevitably blame the framed mission statement. Seems it stopped working. Fearing workers are immune to the lobby poster, one high-ranking leader suggests printing a copy of the mission statement for each worker's office. However, that idea proves only slightly effective since it only reaches employees with offices. Next, they try a pocket-sized laminated card version so employees can carry the mission statement at all times. Management can now sit back and watch for signs that employees are living by these pocket-sized values.

But you already knew the organization's values—that's why you came to work here. You wanted to contribute to the mission, not read about it on a plaque. Your boss was the one who deviated from the values that attracted you. And that deviation forced you out of alignment.

We create mission statements because we want employees to see our big picture. Question is do we see theirs?

## What Do Employees Value?

In the war for talent, companies compete for employer-of-choice designation. However, organizations are slow to recognize the role of values in leadership. Many depend instead on costly fringe benefit packages to attract workers.

There was a time when the most desirable employers were those who offered such perks as incentive pay, paid holidays and vacations, long-term retirement savings plans, employee educational assistance, medical and hospitalization insurance with dental and vision options, and short- and long-term sick leave. Once reserved for employees in worldwide corporations or associated with powerful unions, we now consider these benefits basic.

Not only are these benefits expected, they are usually negotiable, a benefit in and of itself. Candidates commonly haggle for a higher salary, an extra week of vacation, or a shorter waiting period for enrolling in the company 401(k).

Reluctantly, perhaps, some companies add lifestyle enhancing benefits like fitness centers, in-house childcare centers, and take-home catering. Those corporations are attempting to create one-stop campuses, where employees spend the entire workday and still do all their personal errands, too. At such corporate facilities, you park your car in the company garage, deposit your child with the in-house daycare center, take your clothes to the on-site dry-cleaner, leave some shoes at the on-site shoe repair, and drop off a roll of film to be processed by the on-site photo shop. On break, you visit the company library to skim your favorite magazines, you grab a low-fat, low-cholesterol, or low-carbohydrate lunch in the company cafeteria, and while there, you place an order for your family's dinner. After work, you do some Pilates in the fitness center, pick up your shirts, shoes, pictures, dinner, and child, and go home. Carrying everything to your car, you will undoubt-edly complain about the lack of valet parking. Companies incur great expense to provide these lifestyle fringe benefits, hoping to retain comparison-shopping employees and attract window-browsing job candidates. However, lifestyles change. Although some employees might find a daycare center meaningful today, its value will diminish as their children get older.

These days, studies have shown that job seekers are paying closer attention to organizational values, and are less interested in having their companies pay for their lifestyles. Applicants are looking for employers who respect the way they live, and also share their personal values. Organizations are beginning to recog-nize this trend. Here are three examples: At the Timberland Company, management gives employees forty hours paid time off each year to serve in their communities. Employees wanting more time to "give back" can earn paid sabbaticals of up to six months. San Francisco law firm Morrison & Foerster actively demon-strates its strong commitment to diversity. Of the firm's 871 at-torneys, 166 are minorities, including 21 partners. It also has a long history of providing free legal services to indigent persons. In 2003, the firm gave away 102,000 hours of pro bono legal work. Wegmans Food Markets' motto, "Employees first, customers sec-ond," captures the company's passion for customer service. How? Wegmans believes that happy employees mean happy customers. It sponsors year-round leagues in sports from softball to volley-ball, and arranges admission discounts to movies, sporting events, and theme parks. In turn, employees are encouraged to go to un-usual lengths, without seeking permission, to ensure customer satisfaction. Values like these get your company on *Fortune's* list of the "100 Best Companies to Work For."[7]

The movement toward values-based benefits reflects a shift in what workers from every generation value in their employers. But once they've connected to their institution's publicized values, employees expect to see those same values in the organization's leaders. More importantly, they expect their managers to demonstrate those values.

---

# People join an organization.
# They leave a manager.

---

People join an organization, but they leave a manager. Think that's an unfair statement? Granted, some people do resign to go back to school, or because a spouse is transferring. To be certain, some happy people leave. In fact, some happy employees expect even greater happiness elsewhere. However, organizations rarely associate employee turnover with poor managers. Why? In exit interviews, almost all resigning employees avoid "burning any bridges." They spin their reasons for leaving, listing issues like pay, promotion opportunities, or additional benefits. Information garnered from exit interviews is largely irrelevant, and many companies now conduct face-to-face meetings only with departing executives.

Searching for meaningful clues, some companies postpone exit surveys for six months or more after employees have said farewell. The interlude results in feedback that's surprisingly more honest than data obtained in traditional exit interviews. After several months, these same employees are less emotional, because enough time has elapsed for them to weigh objectively their former situations and experiences against their new jobs. Less reliant on positive references from their former employers, they are free to answer honestly when questioned about the reasons for their departure. Not surprisingly, most former employees list poor management as their primary reason for changing jobs.[8]

So, what do people want from their management's leadership?

> # Leadership credibility means consistency between an organization's spoken values and its leaders' actual behavior.

## The Six Vital Integrities of Values-Based Leaders

It bears repeating: employees are searching for leaders with integrity who prove their credibility continuously. In values-based leadership, credibility means consistency between an organization's spoken values and its leaders' actual behavior. Got credibility? Prove it!

To prove your credibility you must repeatedly exhibit your faithfulness to your organization's values by consistently executing the six Vital Integrities.

Understand these six principles, and lead by habitually demonstrating them in action each day, and your leadership will have far greater impact—all because your can't-miss-it credibility underscores your integrity as a leader.

## Accept Challenges and Take Risks

Industries once based their leadership models on the centuries-old notion of organizations as machines, and considered the best-managed workplaces to be those that were machine-like, or orderly and unchanging. In that environment, revered managers held everything under control by keeping their people in line. All hell broke loose if an employee returned five minutes late from a coffee break, or criticized a management decision.

Today, business involves constant change, and to drive change you must leave your comfort zone. Effective leaders must be brave and innovative, try new approaches, and chance failure.

# People can only follow leaders who are moving.

Values-based leaders are risk takers, and more importantly, risk *seekers*, adventurers who position themselves to discover new challenges. They volunteer for the toughest jobs and always question the status quo. Risk seeking separates these leaders from the yesteryear-theory bureaucrats who sit around supervising the work. Why is that important? Leadership is proactive, as people can only follow leaders who are moving.

Values-based leaders courageously question the rules. Why is that a big deal? Let's be honest. The people creating policies are usually the least objective when it comes time to evaluate a rule's effectiveness. So, if the controls have stopped working, if they were bad from the start, or if they conflict with the mission, those rules may need challenging. Who better to question the rules than a leader guided by the organization's values?

Not only must leaders be brave, they must welcome pressure. Take a little risk, add a few challenges, and bake for eight hours in the heat of the workplace: isn't that a great recipe for stress? Most assuredly. But have you ever noticed how some people stress out easily, while others actually seem to embrace the very chaos that causes stress? Research indicates that individual personality differences influence how people appraise and cope with stressful situations. The term *psychological hardiness* refers to a personal attitude that enables some leaders to view challenges as opportunities to learn new things, rather than as threats to fear or avoid. Once you learn to see adversity as an adventure, you will have enough hardiness to weather any crisis.

Values-based leaders teach risk taking to their employees. One way to do that is by celebrating the failures of workers who venture outside their comfort zones. By applauding risk-taking setbacks, these leaders create a safe environment for trial and error, while at the same time encouraging employees to take initiative.

## Master both Listening and Speaking

Of course, leaders must also communicate well. Yet, in their book, *The Leader's Voice*, Boyd Clarke and Ron Crossland describe four fatal assumptions of leadership communication. When leaders make these "fatal assumptions," they assume that when they speak, their listening employees will understand, agree, care, and act accordingly.[9] But what's really happening is that their employees are confused and bewildered by their communication style.

One reason for poor organizational communication is the overuse of jargon, the verbal shorthand intended to streamline dialogue among colleagues. Jargon includes the industrial phrases, buzzwords, euphemisms, abbreviations, and acronyms that compose our professional vocabularies. If all participants in a conversation know the lingo, then using jargon is perfectly acceptable and legitimate. But when jargon is confusing, or used to impress or exclude others, a leader's credibility will be undermined.

Values-based leaders, on the other hand, understand the tremendous power of storytelling. They know that communication is highly effective when they speak to the emotional as well as the intellectual regions of their listeners' minds. Stories are a potent way to reach each listener's emotions while conveying important information. They know that using stories to illustrate the organization's principles allows each employee to absorb their messages in a personal way.

Not only that, but in-person communication occurs visually as well as verbally. Understand this fact and you will master both listening and speaking. As a speaker, you should watch your listeners' body language for signs of comprehension and agreement.

As a listener, you should be engaged in the listening process, and show through your body language your complete focus on the speaker.

Finally, you should know how to hear and make every effort to block your inner voices, hidden biases, or preconceptions from drowning out the speaker's message. By doing so, you will be able to receive not only advice and warnings, but encouragement, as well.

## Live By the Values They Profess

One familiar leadership adage proclaims that managers should assign only those tasks they are willing to do themselves. But integrity and credibility are much too critical to values-based leadership to summarize in trite expressions. If employees detect discrepancy between an organization's spoken values and a leader's actual behavior, they recognize the company's clichés as lip service and their leader as a fraud.

In the hiring process, recruiters introduce aspirants to mutual expectations—how aligning with the organization's values will meet their personal interests and needs. Once on board, employees need constant evidence of compatibility—proof that their leader's values are in alignment with the organization's, and thus, their own. Without frequent confirmation from their leader, employees might decide the organization's values are not what they thought they were.

If they perceive, whether accurately or not, that management changed or somehow misrepresented the values, employees begin to wonder. They may then feel unaligned, lost, and foolish for having trusted the employer. Finally, they withdraw and turn defensive, even cynical. Their initiative diminishes and money becomes their primary motivator. Eventually, they resign.

By proactively demonstrating the correlation between your personal values and those of the organization, you will simultaneously show your employees an allegiance to their values and validate their trust in you.

Professing to value human diversity is about more than tolerance; it's about appreciating individuals for the very things that make them different. Values-based leaders challenge the melting pot notion, where organizations dissolve employee differences and pour their personalities into an ideal corporate mold. Instead, they envision their organizations as quilts, and individuals as patches joined by the fabric of a common purpose. They confront their learned biases and avoid stereotypes.

## Freely Give Away Their Authority

On June 2, 1925, New York Yankee Wally Pipp had a headache. Having played in more games during the previous ten seasons than any other Yankee, Pipp asked manager Miller Huggins for permission to sit out the day's game. In a career that spanned fifteen years, Pipp drove in 997 runs, had six seasons with more than ninety RBIs, and helped the Yankees win three straight pennants. Huggins granted the sick day and replaced Pipp at first base with newcomer Lou Gehrig. Gehrig went on to play in 2,130 straight games. Pipp, despite recovering from the headache, lost his job to the rookie and finished his career with the Cincinnati Reds.[10]

---

## Giving away your authority is a personal challenge that might require confronting common insecurities.

---

Although few leaders know the Wally Pipp story, many worry about facing a similar fate. That's why giving away authority is such a personal challenge. It involves sharing the influence and prestige associated with leadership, and this might require confronting personal insecurities about losing power.

For the most part, people earn their leadership roles by demonstrating other job skills. The promotion brings further scrutiny; in addition to their technical knowledge, new managers must measure up as leaders. As a result, some leaders cling to their old expertise as a safety net.

Once you abandon your concerns about becoming the next Wally Pipp, you will recognize empowering others as its own reward.

In my workshops, someone usually says, "Hey, I'm ready to give away my authority, but my employees are different. They don't want to be empowered." I agree that some employees avoid empowerment. However, when surveyed several months after leaving, former employees cite a lack of challenge, excitement, and flexibility as the second biggest reason they resigned, right behind poor management.[11] Therefore, it is naive for managers to say their employees are resisting empowerment, when many employees are leaving to find more challenge.

Employees truly want to feel important and useful. They hope to contribute, helping shape a worthy endeavor's success. Therefore, you must learn how to empower wisely.

But certain leadership styles always have the opposite effect, leaving employees feeling powerless. Micromanagement, for example, squashes empowerment. Micromanagers mistrust their employees, and have low expectations for their abilities and results. So micromanaged employees "live down to" those expectations, thereby perfectly conforming to the micromanager's views of them.

Leaders never like having their decisions second guessed. But to be effective, leaders need feedback from employees closest to the frontline, even those who challenge authority. Those employees who openly disagree, and risk seeming disrespectful, often bring forth new ideas—or warnings about overlooked problems. Values-based leaders tolerate and embrace mavericks.

Why the emphasis on giving away authority? Giving authority to others demonstrates trust in people. Trusted employees are more effective, creative, and satisfied. And a funny thing happens when you trust people—they trust you back!

## Recognize the Best in Others

Banking is a highly regulated industry, with a slew of forms to complete. Commercial lending is an increasingly competitive banking service. While you're busy completing forms, your competitors are soliciting your clients. So hurry through your paperwork, get back on the street, and make more loans. Good strategy, until the examiners arrive to review your loan documentation. They find forms that are missing information, forms that are missing signatures, and forms that are missing other forms. The loans are good, made to companies with solid financial histories, reliable guarantors, and sufficient collateral. The lenders are obviously qualified underwriters. But the paperwork is a mess!

One solution is to take the most detail-oriented employees you can find and charge them with reviewing the lenders' completed paperwork. They can correct errors so regulators get perfect forms. Works for a while, but your obstinate employees grow intolerant of lenders unable to follow instructions. They wonder why management continues to pay lenders for making mistakes. Forget the quantity and quality of loans generated. They convince management that the lenders have had enough time to master the forms.

Here's an idea. What if you reduce the lenders' pay commensurate with the number of errors found? Now, the lenders are paying more attention. Forms are perfectly filled-out, just ask the meticulous folks still keeping score. Problem is the lenders now spend their time polishing paperwork. So there are fewer new loans and—with less time spent in the underwriting process—more loans that might go unpaid.

A band-aid approach that's unique to banking? Hardly. By focusing attention on their employees' weaknesses, leaders overlook their strengths and take their skills for granted. What if we pay our lenders to do what they do best—like finding new customers, determining the borrower's capability to repay the loan, negotiating pricing, and schmoozing—and pay someone else to do the paperwork? What if we stop frustrating our punctilious types with redundant work—catching and reporting errors—and just pay *them* to fill out the paperwork instead? In other words, what if we use our employees' strengths and work around any weaknesses?

Too many organizations assume employees can become competent in almost anything, if only they try. Companies structure their performance reviews to show employees how they must improve to get ahead. Corporations misspend training budgets on improving employee weaknesses, when they ought to invest in enhancing existing skills.

Values-based leaders recognize that each person's talents are special, and that a person's best opportunity for growth lies in exploiting those strengths. They identify what individual employees do best, encourage workers to shift their focus to those strengths, and help them refine and fortify those abilities. And they show them how to use their talents to bring success to themselves and the organization.

Unfortunately, rather than capitalizing on their employees' strengths, a growing number of organizations are following the latest trends in weakness control, such as ranking, or differentiating, employees into the categories A, B or C, in which A players are their best employees, and C players their worst. Then, all they need to do is fire the C players and hire more A players as replacements. Oh, and did I mention that they must do this every year? Stock analysts love the idea, but human resource professionals—and employment lawyers—detest this systematic method for purging poor performers. And although coveted managers were once those capable of wielding the hatchet without emotion, they will find themselves in higher demand, today, if they can turn those high C or low B employees into valued contributors, instead.

## Have a Vision and Convince Others to Share It

We often describe children as having wild or active imaginations. The best leaders never outgrow their imaginative gift. They hold in their minds pictures of what is possible. Vision is the power to conceive a future that's better than the present.

Good leaders have a vision. *Great* leaders convince others to share their vision by articulating it in memorable and inspirational ways.

An old story relates the role vision plays in making work meaningful. Two stonemasons are working side by side when someone asks them what they are doing. The first mason replies, "I'm cutting stone." The second mason responds, "I'm building a great cathedral." The latter gets inspiration from the work's significance. By seeing backward—first envisioning the finished cathedral, and then the efforts required to create it—the second mason understands how cutting stone contributes to the final goal.

## Most leaders lack the skills needed to share their visions.

The ability to communicate powerfully a vision's significance is critical to values-based leadership, but it requires skills disregarded by almost all business leaders. Why do leaders neglect such important abilities? Because busy leaders find it's easier to read numbers from a financial statement, and conveying information in unrehearsed, jargon-filled language requires little emotion, so they needn't develop dramatic and inspiring presentation skills. However, a workforce increasingly motivated by values needs—indeed expects—inspiration.

A leader might have a unique vision, or embrace a common idea. For instance, many Americans wished for a country free of racial injustice, but the Reverend Dr. Martin Luther King, Jr., vividly envisioned the day when that world would exist. Whether their vision is unique or commonly shared, leaders able to depict a desirable future, like the one King described in his "I Have a Dream" speech, inspire others to follow.

Some people confuse the idea of leaders sharing a values-based vision with the image of prophets, futurists, or renegades attempting to attract followers with radical or extreme ideas. Just the opposite is true. Values-based leaders enlist employees by identifying common interests, and showing them how that shared vision will satisfy mutual needs.

Master the techniques for describing your organization's mission, and you will distinguish yourself as a great leader.

## The Big Muscles

I love golf and, like many avid golfers, I am constantly looking for the secret to lowering my scores. I have attended several golf schools and consulted countless teachers, and although swing theories vary, one thought is consistent among instructors: the bigger a muscle, the more control it exerts in your swing. For example, your arms influence the swing more than your hands, your shoulders more than your arms, and so on. Therefore, execution is easiest when you rely on your biggest muscles. What does that have to do with leadership? I believe that, in leadership, your values are your biggest muscles.

Although it's improbable that every employee's values will match perfectly those of their employer, each person found something in those values that they did connect to, at least in the beginning. So "rehire your employees" every day by showing them, through your values-powered execution of the six Vital Integrities, that your organization's mission statement is more than just a marketing slogan. Do that, and you will help your employees remain aligned and loyal, as well as committed and on board.

# Chapter 1

Values-Based Leaders:
## Accept Challenges and Take Risks

*"To conquer without risk is to triumph without glory."*
-Pierre Corneille

Firefighters and police officers take risks while doing their jobs—risks that place their lives in peril. The rest of us endanger only our egos when taking a risk at work. But whether you jeopardize your physical safety or your pride, accepting such a challenge demonstrates courage. Do your employees really care whether or not you behave courageously? Yes, in fact, they do!

Remember, employees joined your organization because they perceived a connection between their values and the company's values. That bond supplies the meaning and purpose they crave in their jobs, so they expect you to protect those values by fighting senseless rules, defending them against coworker or customer harassment, addressing the poor performance of employees who habitually slack off, and standing up against corporate injustice.

How you respond to their expectations influences not only how much, but even *if* your employees will trust you at all. Studies have shown that most employees distrust their organization's leaders. And if your employees regard you with skepticism, or even suspicion, you will need to first earn their trust, and then actively maintain it.

But how do you go about acquiring employee trust? Every time you do something that demonstrates adherence to your organization's values, each employee who either witnesses or hears about it will subconsciously give you a deposit in an imaginary "trust fund." At first, those deposits receive what banks call provisional credit. If there is uncertainty about a deposit, banks give good customers temporary credit, conditional on its verification. Employees grant trust the same way. When crediting you for demonstrating the organization's values, your employees give you the benefit-of-the-doubt, until you prove unworthy of their trust.

## What Kind of Risks?

Although your job might not involve entering burning buildings or facing armed suspects, you still need courage to lead effectively. Here are some classes of risk taking that will make your "trust fund" grow.

### Admitting Ignorance

Saying "I don't know" is risky, especially when people defer to your experience and expertise. In his book, *Only the Paranoid Survive*, Intel CEO Andrew Grove described how competition drove his company to abandon the memory chip business and enter the microprocessor field. During the makeover, Grove realized he needed to learn more about the software industry. So he arranged meetings with the heads of software companies and asked them to share their knowledge. "This entailed some personal risk," Grove acknowledged. "It required swallowing my pride and admitting how little I knew about their business." Nevertheless, Grove took lots of notes during those meetings. Back at

Intel, he asked his internal experts to explain the meaning of all the information he'd gathered.

Admitting his ignorance meant risking the respect of industry peers and employees, but the learning process was critical to Intel's future. "After all," wrote Grove, "how we would do our job depended on the plans, thoughts, desires and visions of the software industry."[1]

Leadership requires the courage to surround yourself with employees who are potentially better at their jobs than you are at yours. By owning up to a lack of knowledge and deferring to their expertise, you will show workers that you are willing to risk your pride in order to get the job done.

## Pushing for Change

Risk taking often involves challenging tradition. Writing in the October 2000 edition of the popular business magazine *Fast Company*, former U.S. labor secretary Robert Reich proclaimed, "In a time of constant change, one thing hasn't changed: Organizations are still resistant to change. The change agent of the old economy worked in an environment where incremental change was all that was needed—and all that was tolerated." Reich also noted that being a change agent these days is inadequate. "Change today demands the change insurgent."[2]

> ## Corner office bureaucrats might be sadly out of touch with technology, customer demands, and workforce capabilities.

Here's the significance of Reich's observations. People with authoritative titles—or their minions—customarily drive change downward. But bureaucrats nestled in their corner offices are less in touch with technology, customer wishes, or workforce capabilities than employees who are working on the front lines. For a company to remain competitive, new ideas must originate from all levels of the corporate hierarchy, but driving change from below is often a high-risk, low-reward game. Rising up to promote change might earn you an ill-favored reputation as a rebel. Policy makers—especially those entrenched at the top of a bureaucracy—are probably the people who established the very practices you are trying to change. Having the audacity to suggest improving or abandoning long-standing procedures is politically dangerous, and, quite often, when suggestions are well-received, the bureaucrats take credit for those ideas, anyway.

So is it really worth the risk? Yes, if the changes you advocate are equally important to the values of your employees and your organization. Those common values provide workers with the meaning and connection they need in their jobs. Pushing for changes that uphold your organization's values demonstrates your credibility.

## Challenging Bad Decisions

I once openly criticized the unimaginable way senior management terminated an administrative assistant. The decision to eliminate her position was sound, but her boss quite visibly botched the process. Management set a termination date three months out, intending to give her time to find another position internally. But because her boss was uncomfortable delivering the bad news, he waited to up-end her life until it was too late. To top it off, her severance package was contingent on her signing a one-year noncompete agreement, highly unusual for an employee at that level. The company was mistreating a loyal veteran employee for all to see.

I called on her supervisor—who was coincidentally my boss—to acknowledge his mishandling, and to intervene in having the noncompete prerequisite set aside. He was unwilling to intercede, so I scrambled against the clock. I argued with the policy makers in Human Resources, asked managers from other departments for projects to buy her additional time, and despairingly sought intervention from the board chair. Alas, the message was clear: Stay out of it!

The next day, the president summoned me to his office for admonishment. "Where in your job description," he chastened, "is it written that you're responsible for protecting all the employees of this company?"

"It's implied," I responded, "in my title of manager."

## Who are *you* to question a bad decision?

Although I was unsuccessful in this battle, my efforts showed my employees that I would wage war on their behalf against similar betrayals. It proved that we shared common values—the values of fairness, and dignity, and accountability.

Who are you to question your boss's bad decisions? Says Grove, "If you are in middle management, don't be a wimp. Don't sit on the sidelines waiting for the senior people to make a decision so that later on you can criticize them over a beer—'My God, how could they be so dumb?' Your time for participating is now."[3]

## Blowing the Whistle

In August 2001, Enron vice president Sherron Watkins warned board chair Kenneth Lay that the company was using shady accounting practices—specifically, off-the-books deals secured only by devalued Enron stock. In May 2002, FBI staff attorney Coleen Rowley wrote a memo to agency director Robert Mueller. In it, she described how officials ignored warnings from the Minneapolis field office about Zacarias Moussaoui, a French-Moroccan enrolled in an area flight school, before the events of September 11, 2001. In June 2002, WorldCom internal auditor Cynthia Cooper disclosed to its board's audit committee how the company had covered up $3.8 billion in losses through deceitful bookkeeping methods. *TIME* magazine named these three courageous women its 2002 "Persons of the Year."[4]

But most workers are far too faint-hearted for whistle blowing. Too many exhibit an unquestioning, even fearful, reverence for authority. Others equate goodness with obedience; accordingly, they defer moral choices to outside authorities—their parents, teachers, or bosses. Others worry about earning unwanted reputations as tattlers.

Everyone wants to be a team player, especially when hierarchical rank looms threatening overhead, imposing its unethical demands. Many organizations require new hires to sign away their rights to moral judgment—as well as their right to a jury trial—in exchange for salary and perks. Noncompete agreements, increasingly common in management compensation packages, trap professionals into tolerating moral misconduct. Just what kind of a "team" is this, anyway?

Their bravery in risking everything for their values sets Watkins, Rowley, and Cooper apart from most leaders. Each initially believed she had discovered trouble unforeseen by senior management, and expected her organization's leaders to not only show appreciation, but to intervene. When cover-ups ensued instead, each took it upon herself to rectify the bad behavior; she stepped up and did the right thing.

"There is a price to be paid," says Cooper, adding, "There have been times that I could not stop crying." That makes her efforts all the more remarkable.

## Addressing Performance Issues

Several years ago, I had to confront an employee about a recurring tardiness problem. It was far from my first disciplinary conversation, having dealt over time with everything from below-standard work performance to outright theft, and I had developed a thick skin for such managerial interventions. But this was different.

The woman provided administrative services for an entire department with two dozen sales and support professionals. She was uncommonly efficient. Once, our department relocated to newly constructed office space over a three-day weekend. When the staff returned from the holiday, expecting to begin emptying boxes and getting settled, they discovered everything put away and neatly organized. We found files stored and labeled; fax machines and printers plugged in, cabled, and functioning; kitchen cleaning supplies lined up under the lunchroom sink. All thanks to our administrative assistant's frenzied weekend efforts and personal initiative.

Despite her tremendous organizing abilities, she was consistently late for work. One day she would be five minutes late. The next day, ten minutes. The day after that, a half hour. She was aware of the problem; when she was late, she always stayed after work hours to make up the time. But it was my duty to explain our expectation of a timely morning arrival. After all, her coworkers were coming to work on time and I—notwithstanding my thick skin—had wrestled with my unease long enough.

It was then that I learned how individuals with a disease called Obsessive Compulsive Disorder suffer. After telling me about her affliction, she described how it affected her ability to get to work on time. She would be ready to leave the house and, at the last minute, feel the urge to make sure she had turned off the stove. Back at the door, she would experience a need to straighten the cushions on the couch. Then, the stove would beckon again. Some days it took half an hour for the compulsions to subside.

Turns out my hesitancy to tackle the tardiness problem had made things more difficult on us all. She had sensed my concern for some time, and waiting for me to say something only added to her anxiety. Some of her coworkers were wondering, too. Was I being too lax, or applying the rules unfairly?

Understanding her issue enabled me to provide a flexible schedule and help a valued employee. What took me so long?

## Managers tend to blame themselves for an employee's performance problems.

Someone once told me that firing people gets easier the more you do it. That's probably true when firing dishonest employees. But addressing performance problems is usually quite a personal challenge. Firing people over performance can be gut-wrenching.

If you are like most managers, you tend to blame yourself for an employee's disappointing performance. After all, you hired this underperformer. Did you overlook something or make an error of judgment? Did you fail to provide enough training and motivation? What does firing this person say about your leadership abilities? Perhaps there's still a chance for rehabilitation. Maybe you ought to give the employee—and yourself—a little more time.

Fact is, as a leader, you will inevitably have to fire someone. When the time comes, avoid delay. And be direct. I have watched managers tiptoe around so gingerly in termination meetings that doomed employees have finally asked, "Are you firing me?"

When employees fail to live up to their responsibilities, display the courage to live up to yours.

## Volunteer to Go First

Robert Galvin, board chair and CEO of Motorola for nearly thirty years, once gave the following definition of leadership: "Leadership is going first in a new direction—and being followed."[5]

My former coworker Jim Stram and I once attended a leadership summit sponsored by our company for managers from several cities. One exercise involved an outside ropes course. Secured in our climbing gear and safely tethered by belays, our challenge was to ascend thirty feet above the ground and demonstrate our physical agility by crossing various rope bridges strung between utility poles. To accommodate the large number of participants, there were two identical courses, built side by side. Jim and I headed off for different courses.

When my group's instructor called for a volunteer to go first, I looked over at the adjacent course and saw Jim already climbing. He is a strapping former athlete, so seeing Jim leading his group up the ladder was not hard to predict. But, whether I was inspired by Jim's bravery, or worried that he would upstage me, I found myself ignoring my fear of heights and raising my hand.

Soon, I was nervously navigating along the course, swinging between Burma loops, clawing my way across a cargo net, and traversing a balance beam. Then, on an exercise called the hour glass, I found myself hanging upside down, clinging to a rope, and trying desperately to forestall what I imagined would prove an embarrassing rescue. But with encouragement from my team-mates and suggestions from the instructor, I managed to right myself and finish the course. Exhausted, exhilarated, and dripping with sweat, I returned to the ground and joined Jim sitting under a nearby tree.

"Wasn't that awesome?" I asked.

"I didn't do it," he responded.

"What? But, I saw you going up the ladder."

"Yeah," he said, "I got halfway up the ladder, but my fear of heights kept me from going any higher. So I came back down."

Later that day, course facilitators persuaded participants to acknowledge any positive influences they received from one another during the exercise. My group thanked me for showing the courage to go first and lead our team onto the course. Many said they gained inspiration by my action. But Jim provided the initial inspiration by disregarding his personal aversion to heights to be the first to try. Without realizing it, Jim helped me overcome my fear and, as a result, inspired others as well.

---

## "Leadership matters most when it is least clear what course should be followed."
Michael Useem[6]

---

As a leader, you must summon the courage to chart the course, venture into the unknown, challenge defeat, and risk disappointment. Your initiative will encourage others. Whether you risk personal safety or personal embarrassment for the sake of your values, by taking that risk you inspire others to follow.

## Trusting Your Employees

Employees want to have influence in their jobs. In other words, they want you to leave them alone and trust them to do their work.

But many managers find trusting their employees highly anxiety-provoking because of the risk involved. The urge to peek over their shoulders, or even do the work themselves, is great. Some managers live in fear that their employees will mess up, produce substandard work, and ultimately cost them their jobs.

As workers, we receive praise for our hands-on attention to detail. But in leadership, we consider that micromanagement. For some, a natural propensity to take action—or take over—conquers the willingness to empower their workers. (There's more on micromanagement in chapter 4.) As you will—sooner or later—learn, it all revolves around trust.

Many leaders consider themselves risk takers. Fact is, most leadership risk taking is by assignment: a higher authority delegates a task outside your comfort zone, creating a risky challenge for you to meet. But if you wait for an invitation to take risks, your chances of earning employee trust are limited, and building up a permanent balance in your "trust fund" will take years. The real time for action is now.

## Risk Taking and Risk Seeking

Once upon a time, when there was honor among soldiers, prisoners of war were duty-bound to make every effort to escape. In fact, attempting escape was part of what many considered the noble game of war, rather than a punishable wartime act.

In his book, *A Prisoner's Duty,* Robert C. Doyle describes four different escaper personalities. Prisoners who resist captivity at all costs, called "tigers" in the Korean War, start looking for ways to escape immediately after their capture. Others seize opportunities that present themselves, gambling on a spur-of-the-moment break. Some need the comfort found in forming partnerships and planning joint escapes. Then there are those Doyle calls the "Great Escapers" who organize groups of prisoners and mastermind mass escapes.[7]

Unassertive prisoners usually need provocation in order to attempt an escape, like experiencing or witnessing cruel acts by their captors. On the other hand, "tigers" find inspiration in their sense of duty. By the same token, in business, some leaders respond to assigned challenges, while those who resemble tiger escapees look for their own ways of fulfilling their organization's mission.

Imagine that your company's mission statement says protecting the environment is a core value. In the past three months, you've repeatedly suggested production improvements to your immediate supervisor that will reduce carbon dioxide emissions. Although acknowledging the benefit of the changes, your manager has failed to act on your suggestions, or make your ideas known to the CEO. You wonder if the manager still shares the organization's commitment to the environment, and worry increasingly about unnecessary harmful emissions continuing to occur each day that your suggestions go unheard.

## How we perceive threats influences our risk-taking decisions.

What actions should you take? Should you take advantage of the CEO's open-door policy (he publicly and repeatedly says that his door is "always open") and present your ideas directly, in person? Or should you consider the open-door speech just more insincere CEO rhetoric, and continue making your case to your supervisor? Perhaps you should put your ideas in a memo to your boss and copy the CEO. Or should you wait for a chance meeting with the CEO to mention your ideas informally?

Each choice has risks. There is the possibility of political fall-out in going around your boss to the CEO. But continuing to challenge the status quo with your supervisor, even though it maintains the chain of command, could get you labeled a malcontent. The transparent memo method carries much the same risk as a direct approach. And waiting for a chance encounter to tell the CEO about your ideas seems safe, but what if the opportunity proves elusive? How can you make the right decision?

## Assessing Risk

You are undoubtedly holding a position of leadership because you possess political astuteness, and have learned to choose your battles wisely. How we select our fights depends on how we evaluate their risk.

First, we weigh our chances of success. The greater the likelihood of success, the more willing we are to take the risk. Likewise, if we consider our chances for succeeding remote, we will probably avoid the risk. If your assumptions are tested and you are certain your ideas will reduce emissions, you are more likely to sidestep the boss. But if your proposal is a bit of a gamble, partnering with your supervisor is a more cautious but wiser approach.

Next, we measure the importance of success. The more important we perceive success, the less eager we are to take a risk. Let's say you are a basketball player, during a time out with two seconds left in the game. Your team has the ball and an opportunity for one last shot. "Who wants to try it?" asks the coach. If your team is ahead by ten points, you may say, "Give me the ball." If successful, your shot will make the highlight film. But if you miss, your team will still win. Now, what if the score is even?

Maybe you still volunteer to take the shot. Score the basket and you are a hero. Miss and your team has a chance to win in over-time. However, if your team is down by a point, and the shot's outcome determines whether your team wins or loses, you may cautiously resist the urge to step forward.

We also gauge how much control we have in the outcome. If you believe the CEO will listen to your ideas, you risk the possible backlash of making an end run around your immediate supervisor. But if you expect the CEO will defer to your supervisor, you'll probably keep your ideas to yourself.

Finally, we assess our own skill. The more confident we are in our own abilities, the more enthusiastic we are to try something. If you are certain of making that last-second shot, you'll say, "Give me the ball, coach!" If you consider yourself an expert in carbon dioxide emissions, you know you are qualified to recommend your measures directly to the CEO.

Although those assessments are helpful for choosing our battles wisely, we make them out of selfishness. Will I embarrass myself by failing? Will my teammates dislike me if I miss the final shot? Will I feel inferior and powerless if my boss overrides my decision? Do I have what it takes to pull off the risk—or will I expose my limitations? And those assessments, by focusing on personal consequences, inhibit us from taking risks.

I would suggest that a values-based assessment should override all other assessments of risk. That is: does taking this risk demonstrate your adherence to the organization's values, or not?

For instance, since your mission statement specifies protecting the environment as a key value, your suggestions are appropriate to the mission. Perhaps you've long preached the importance of reducing carbon dioxide emissions. You've instilled this value in your staff. You have a reputation as the company expert in environmental control technologies. Of course, you also want to advance your career, and you are well aware that your supervisor's recommendation will directly influence your success.

You are confident your ideas are sound, your abilities enormous, but your career aspirations, and their dependency on a favorable nod from your supervisor, make success especially important.

From a personal assessment, there is greater risk in going directly to the CEO. It might be best to uphold the sacred chain of command by reiterating your recommendations to your supervisor. If your employees are unaware of your situation, or that you've considered going over your manager's head, preserving the status quo will still maintain the level of trust they have in you, since they won't know you're not living up to your stated values and theirs, not to mention your company's.

Now apply the values-based assessment. Imagine the message you will send your employees by taking the riskier road. Remember, many employees were attracted to the organization because of its focus on the environment. That alignment process persists after employees come on board, as they continue to observe and interpret their leaders' behavior. They look for constant affirmation that the leaders' stated values are in alignment with the organization's, and thus, their own. By choosing to take a risk, you will demonstrate your conviction to environmental protection, and your commitment to the organization's mission. And your employees will notice your integrity.

## Be a risk seeker.

Should you be a risk seeker or a risk taker? Risk takers wait for chances to do the right thing to arise naturally. Values-based leaders actively seek out opportunities to do the right thing— thereby converting their provisional credit to permanent trust.

The choice is clear: you must be a risk seeker. You must prove your credibility by proactively looking for opportunities to demonstrate courage, and thereby earn employee trust.

## Challenging the Rules

An old saying proclaims that leaders prefer asking for forgiveness rather than begging for permission. Of course, so do teenagers and six-year-olds! What's the difference? Children act largely in their own interest, while we expect our leaders to operate in the organization's best interest. Fact is, as a leader, you may have to challenge some rules.

Jeff Bezos is the founder and CEO of Amazon.com. Obsessed with innovation, Bezos sees corporate hierarchy as an obstacle to creativity. That's why the company offers an employee incentive called the "Just-Do-It" award. Recipients are workers who think through the situation, follow their instincts, and act on Amazon.com's behalf without begging for the boss's permission first. Many organizations would punish those actions. Most would find encouraging that behavior akin to spreading a deadly corporate plague. However, in an article about Amazon.com in the May 26, 2003, issue of *Fortune*, Fred Vogelstein quotes Bezos as saying, "the cure—to encourage people to always ask for permission—is worse than the disease."[8]

Mention challenging the rules, and many people immediately worry about lawlessness, ethical violations, human rights infringements, or breached bargaining table agreements. But values-based leadership inspires adherence to an organization's principles. In effect, the six-year-old-child analogy is a good one; parents instill values and morals in their children, and then trust them to go off on their own and do the right thing. Leaders like Bezos provide a values-based framework within which employees have the freedom to act responsibly, without having to ask permission.

Rules exist in the organization's best interest. For instance, rules outlining the organization's expectations concerning workplace issues like harassment, conflicts of interest, and violence, provide the compass for day-to-day decision making and link the organization's values to standards of professional conduct. But some rules may be outdated because the company established them long ago, back when management was all about keeping everything stagnant.

In his book, *Clicks and Mortar*, David Pottruck described how a team at Charles Schwab challenged the rules for resolving customer complaints.[9] Although only a fraction of the millions of monthly transactions Schwab employees handled resulted in complaints, outstanding problems were piling up and response times were averaging longer than two weeks. The team searched for ways to shorten resolution time by a few days, which they accomplished by convincing front-line workers to give greater urgency to customer complaints. Inspired, the team next strived to shorten response time even further, and began looking under every procedural rock.

The company procedures called for acknowledging all complaints in writing. When one team member questioned the need for such formality, veteran employees maintained that the letters were legally required. But, sensing the letters were more tradition than a matter of law, the team challenged the company's rule and discovered that the regulation was outdated. By eliminating the letter, they shortened the resolution time to a mere five days.

The team then set its sights on a previously unimaginable possibility: could the company respond to these complaints within forty-eight hours? Pottruck, the company's co-CEO, writes, "This question called for a break-through. When a question like this is asked, people start to question all the givens, all their preconceived notions and the fundamental 'rules of the game.'"

And question they did. In fact, they questioned the actual rules for their assignment. Was their purpose to speed up complaint resolution, or to improve overall customer satisfaction? After all, customers wanted their problems resolved quickly, but—more importantly—they wanted them decided in their favor. After careful analysis, the team concluded that employees could settle 80 percent of the complaints immediately, in the customer's favor, for less than it cost to research most problems. According to Pottruck, "This is no longer about incrementally solving a problem, it is about redefining the problem entirely, [so] people begin to challenge even their own assumptions."

## Ask why, why, why.

Challenging the rules is a far cry from breaking the law. But it *is* about examining policies, procedures, and practices hindering the organization's mission. Challenging the rules is unrelated to violating ethics. But it *is* about questioning authority, if said authority asks you to compromise your morals. *Take these documents down the hall and shred them.* Challenging the rules runs counter to infringing on someone's rights. But it *is* about confronting people who show disrespect for others by making offensive racial or ethnic remarks, and about disobeying the convention that says the customer is always right, even when the customer is harassing our employees. Finally, challenging the rules is different from breaching agreements made at the bargaining table. But it *is* about negotiating in good faith, disregarding strategies like asking for 10 percent when you will settle for 3 percent, or offering 1 percent when you are prepared to go to three.

Challenging the rules means questioning the status quo. Ricardo Semler, CEO of Brazil-based Semco, described his company's philosophy in his book, *The Seven-Day Weekend*. "If we have a cardinal strategy that forms the bedrock for all our practices, it may be this: Ask why. Ask it all the time, ask it any day, every day, and always ask it three times in a row."[10]

Semler admits that asking questions is unnatural. Grownups teach us early in life that asking too many questions is impolite. And asking questions could betray our ignorance. But by challenging useless and out-of-date rules, leaders are adhering to their organization's values, living up to their responsibilities, and upholding the trust their employees place in them.

And, as Semler reminds us, organizations must avoid what he calls "calcified" thinking, "that state of mind where ideas have become so hardened that they're no longer of any use." That strategy works for his company. In ten years, Semco's annual revenues grew from $35 million to $212 million. "Employees must be free to question, to analyze, to investigate; and a company must be flexible enough to listen to the answers. Those habits are the key to longevity, growth, and profit."

## Embracing Chaos

Ever notice how some people handle stress better than others do? Research shows that personality differences predict how people evaluate and cope with stress.

In the late 1970s, and well into the 1980s, psychologists Suzanne Kobasa and Salvatore Maddi studied the impact from job-related stress on 430 executives at Illinois Bell Telephone. The company was undergoing an enormous divestiture mandated by deregulation, and in just one year cut its workforce of 26,000 in half. Nearly two-thirds of the executives studied showed significant breakdowns in performance (burnout, poor reviews, or demotions) and medical health (heart attacks, strokes, obesity, or depression). The remaining third, while experiencing the same stress levels and disruption as their peers, maintained health and performance, actually embracing the upheavals. Those who thrived possessed what Drs. Kobasa and Maddi called *psychological hardiness.*[11]

To comprehend hardiness fully, we must first understand what stress is. Stress is a physiological reaction triggered by a perceived threat to our physical or psychological safety. Our bodies are equipped with an inherent response system that prepares us to fight or flee whenever danger is apparent. Adrenaline releases into our bloodstream. Our heart starts beating faster, our breathing becomes more rapid, blood pressure increases, and blood sugar levels rise. Blood shifts to our peripheral muscles, making them tense and ready for action.

Think about a time when you were driving and another car suddenly appeared in the road, forcing you to slam on your breaks. Do you remember your vice-like grip on the steering wheel, the feeling of your heart pounding, and the several minutes it took to regain your composure again afterwards? Or consider how firm your muscles felt during a recent workout at the gym, and how that firmness mysteriously went away before you got home. In both instances, your body was responding to physical threats, whether by the rush of adrenaline in the near accident, or by shifting blood to your arm and leg muscles to help lift heavy weights.

Psychological threats are more likely to trigger your workplace stress than physical perils. Your body responds as if the dangers are physical, except mental anxiety replaces muscular tension. Unrealistic predictions distort your thought process and, in turn, negatively affect both your health and productivity. Like your physical reaction, your emotional response is to prepare for the worst, limiting your ability to reason and accurately process information. *I'll never get this problem resolved, I'll lose this job, and I'll never find another one.*

---

## Our physical and emotional reactions to stress exist to prepare us for the worst.

---

Why does your body react to workplace stress the same way it does to a physical threat? Because your brain tells your body what is dangerous. And if your brain perceives danger, rightly or wrongly, it alerts your body to launch the stress response process.

If the stress persists, or if certain stressors become chronic, the body prepares for the extended threat. In converts fat and sugar into fuel. Blood platelets become sticky so wounds will clot faster if you get injured. The brain releases endorphins to ease potential pain. The body must divert energy from long-term maintenance systems, like digestion and the immune response, to deal with the prolonged danger. The result is an enhanced vulnerability to illness.

Persistent stress at work can result from major changes, such as mergers and acquisitions. Lingering stress can occur during difficult projects, or in peak business seasons. Intimidating or negative managers can also create unrelenting stress.

Kobasa and Maddi found that psychologically hardy individuals perceive stress very differently. By viewing stressful situations more realistically, hardy people are able to block the debilitating physical response. For example, people committed to and involved in their work are more apt to perceive stress as interesting and meaningful. Without the threatening perceptions, individuals with committed attitudes are free to actively address and overcome stressful events.

One highly committed individual is Vonnie Bell, an administrative supervisor for the commercial credit subsidiary of a *Fortune* 500 manufacturer. The unit thrived as one of the parent company's most successful enterprises, delivering consistent earnings and winning the prestigious Malcolm Baldrige National Quality Award. Its reputation for promoting from within attracted success-minded professionals like Vonnie. However, when the corporation unexpectedly announced its decision to sell the subsidiary, many workers fled. Vonnie stayed, continuing to work hard while hoping for a position with the eventual new owner. But the company went unsold. It began divesting its loan and lease portfolios separately, sinking any opportunity for a job with another owner. Vonnie remained, still contributing outstanding efforts and hoping for an eventual transfer to the parent corporation.

Like the hardy leaders in the Kobasa and Maddi study, Vonnie outperformed many of her coworkers despite facing identical stress. While attending *The Leading from the Heart Workshop*, she likened her situation to reading a book and realizing midway through that the story is dull and uninteresting. Some people simply close the book, unwilling to waste time reading a boring story. Others feel impelled to finish what they started. Vonnie described herself as the latter. By continuing with the company and helping it complete its asset sale, Vonnie proclaimed her decision not only to finish the book, but also to help write its final chapter.

Thanks to a strong commitment to her work, Vonnie was better able to buffer stress than her alienated peers were. Although some coworkers resented the company for causing their misfortunes, she found gratification in helping it sell each asset for a profit. "I've actually enjoyed this experience," says Vonnie, whose committed attitude allowed her to perceive threats realistically, and forgo sending unnecessary warning signals to her body's stress response system. Has it paid off? "My accomplishments, coupled with my dedication and loyalty, have allowed me to become very visible to key people within this organization," says Vonnie. "But whatever happens, I'll have this meaningful experience behind me and highly regarded references to help me find my next career."

Kobasa and Maddi noticed that individuals also perceive stress more accurately when they believe their personal efforts can actively influence life's events. People adapt to change best when they understand the control they have over their environments.

Vice Admiral James Stockdale was the senior ranking U.S. prisoner of war in Hanoi during the Vietnam War. Shot down over North Vietnam during his second combat tour, Stockdale spent eight years in captivity. His captors tortured him repeatedly, kept him in leg irons for two years, and locked him in solitary confinement for four years.

In his book, *Good to Great*, Jim Collins discusses his interview with Stockdale, in which the veteran fighter pilot described the type of prisoner who succumbed in captivity.[12] Those were the detainees who believed they would return home by Thanksgiving, then Christmas, then Easter, but their spirits weakened with each passing milestone, until their hearts were permanently broken. In what he calls "The Stockdale Paradox," Collins summarizes Stockdale's lesson: maintain faith that you will prevail in the end, but have the discipline to confront the brutal reality.

Hardy individuals realize they control their own destiny, as well as the ultimate impact stressful events will have on their lives. Stockdale believed his release was inevitable. But more importantly, he was determined that his experience positively define his future life. Hardy leaders understand how they contribute in meaningful ways to society and to the lives of others. Through his extensive writing and teaching, Stockdale has taught people how to prevail with dignity against any adversity.

## When we treat stress and chaos as challenging, we avoid launching our built-in "fight or flight" response.

As Kobasa and Maddi witnessed, when we view stressful events as challenging, they become normal aspects of life. When chaos is expected and welcomed, we can perceive it as stimulating, if not a hidden opportunity for personal development.

I learned the importance of looking at stressful situations as challenging from one of my former employees. Senior management became concerned with an increase in customer service complaints, especially because some of those grievances were reaching the CEO's desk. Management was worried about losing existing clients, but realized that addressing service glitches was cutting into the sales staff's new business development efforts. The CEO wanted to establish a centralized problem resolution team to whom salespeople could refer all customer problems. My experience in information technology, operations, and sales made me the boss's first choice to lead the initiative.

At first, all I could imagine was the stress of dealing with the growing problem list. Yet I knew my experience made me a good choice, and I began envisioning the interesting challenge of attacking problems that only my team could resolve.

I quickly compiled a list of potential team members and held a recruitment meeting. Like me, most were initially uneasy about enlisting. But eventual team member Mike Van Zile spoke up, using a wonderful analogy to explain our challenge. Mike correlated our quality issues to those facing the major American car manufacturers in the 1970s and 1980s. Recalling how those companies consequently lost business to rivals Honda, Toyota, and Mazda, Mike said every problem we unraveled would help prevent customers from fleeing to our competition. It was the perfect challenge these customer service-oriented professionals needed to hear, and each identified candidate volunteered. We nicknamed ourselves the "Saturn Project" after the company General Motors created to compete with the imports. Mike's description made the project provocative, making his teammates less intimidated by the huge number of problems we faced, and more concerned with establishing a successful resolution rate.

Leaders must be hardy. But how can you increase your hardiness?

Start by rethinking perceived threats to remove any accompanying distortions. We accept familiar thoughts as certain, but rather than imagining the worst—that your boss will fire you, if a problem goes unresolved—restate the thought and make it into something you are also convinced is true. *I know I'm a vital employee and that I'm needed here. I'm unlikely to lose my job if I cannot resolve this. And even if they do fire me, I'm a talented person with valuable skills, and there are many employers needing someone like me.*

For many of us, work is our identity, our role, and our place in the world. We describe ourselves with such expressions as *I am an accountant* or *I am an insurance agent.* Those statements limit our personal identity and self-value to our work roles, placing our destiny in our employer's hands. In fact, our jobs are just one role of many in our lives. You need to recognize that work is something you do, rather than someone you are. Start by replacing the phrase *I am an accountant* with *I work in accounting,* and notice the immediate sense of control you gain.

The key to increasing hardiness is altering your impression of your own abilities to handle stress. One idea is to precede negative thoughts and statements with the words "up until now." *Up until now, I was incapable of solving this problem.* That approach acknowledges the past while providing permission to change old thought habits.

One workshop participant declared herself "closet hardy." She explained how she successfully masked her negative reactions to stress at work, waiting until she was home to lose control. That participant confused hardiness with acting. The secret to hardiness is not in hiding your emotions, but in avoiding the perceptions that cause stress in the first place.

One added benefit to becoming hardy: studies indicate that psychological hardiness plays a major role in slowing down the aging process. Many authorities on aging believe that coping and dealing with stress positively will help you live a longer, healthier life.[13]

So be hardy!

## Hardiness and Intimidating Managers

In military or police academies, drill instructors help recruits understand how to follow a chain of command. They do this by creating so much stress that unseasoned recruits fail. Failure forces them to obey those above them in command, without thinking. What these drill instructors understand, and what intimidating managers are seemingly incapable of comprehending, is that bullying causes stress, and stress interferes with performance. Therefore, the more leaders intimidate, the greater the likelihood that their charges will make mistakes.

Drill instructors employ methods that make even the hardiest individuals feel stress. For instance, they insist that trainees assume the position of *attention* before following instructions—

before executing any command. If you forget, and are unlucky enough to try turning *about face* while you are still *at ease*, you can expect immediate humiliation.

Try standing at attention: remain erect and motionless, eyes to the front, shoulders back, arms at your sides, fingers curled as if holding a roll of dimes in each hand, heels together, both feet turned outward. This hardly feels like a position of readiness. Can you imagine a tennis player awaiting a serve in that position? How can we expect someone with such a rigid stance to respond effectively to instructions?

What a great way to ensure that your workers perform poorly. After all, what is attention? Break down the word and it sounds like *at-tension*. And when people are tense, mistakes happen.

This exercise teaches workshop participants the importance of employee hardiness and why managing by intimidation prevents workers from performing at their best. Again, drill instructors understand stress and use it to their advantage. Intimidating managers falsely believe fear can produce good results.

---

## Fail more—take more risks.

---

## Failure

People venturing outside their comfort zones by seeking risks will fail a significant portion of the time. Suffice it to say, if you are not failing, you are probably not taking enough risks. Experienced risk seekers, having tried, failed, and returned to try again, are wiser, hardier, more creative, and better qualified to know what—and what not—to try next.

Risk-seeking leaders view setbacks as necessary feedback. However, leaders must understand how their employees view failure.

Remember our internal risk assessment process? We began by evaluating the likelihood of success. Next, we measured the situation's importance. We judged how much control, if any, we have over the outcome. We assessed our own competencies. And as values-based leaders, we considered how taking the risk demonstrated our commitment to our organization's values.

When they fail, employees add new elements to their risk-taking assessment process. After failing, employees tend to concoct common assumptions about themselves that will impact their future risk-taking behavior.

Some people associate results with competence. Therefore, they assume failure reveals incompetence, while also indicating that subsequent failures are more probable. Employees who make this assumption when they fail become wary of taking future risks.

Others will correlate an outcome with luck or odds, and assume success makes eventual failure more probable. *Wow, I could never do that again.* Employees who make this assumption also believe the reverse—that failure makes future success more likely. *I can't be wrong all the time.* These are predictable conclusions, but are they accurate?

On the other hand, repeated success tends to nurture complacency, overconfidence, and negligence, thus increasing the likelihood of human errors. But failure drives us to tweak and fine-tune our approaches in order to avoid additional mistakes. The trouble with all of this thinking is that it either discourages risk taking, or it encourages gambling on the wrong risks. To help employees reach their full initiative-taking potential, you must teach them how to deal with their setbacks and defeats.

As a leader, you must do two things to improve your employees' perceptions about failure. First, you must guard against making similar assumptions about employees when they fail. Refrain from expecting those who stumble to fail in all subsequent risks. Avoid concluding that employees fail simply because of rotten breaks. Second, you must provide feedback and coaching when employees experience failure.

Why? When employees are afraid to fail, they are afraid to try. Babe Ruth hit 714 career home runs, but he struck out 1,330 times. During his career with the Chicago Bulls, Michael Jordan converted 51 percent of all shots he took from the field; in other words, he missed half his shots. We consider both athletes superstars because of their successes, even though they technically failed at least as often as they succeeded. But if Babe Ruth counted strikeouts rather than adding up his home runs, he might have stopped swinging. Had Michael Jordan hesitated before each shot, calculating his odds, he might not have made a shot at all. You want your "Babe Ruth" employees swinging for the bleachers and your "Michael Jordans" taking their jump shots.

## Forgive and forget?

As leaders, we have a natural tendency to forgive and forget when employees fail. After all, beating up employees for failing is insensitive. It might also be counterproductive—when failures are associated with behaviors you are trying to encourage, like risk taking. So how can you forgive your employees for failing without losing an opportunity to drive home important lessons? Do it by celebrating!

## Celebrating Failures

I still recall my experience learning to ride a two-wheel bicycle. One afternoon, my father removed the training wheels, gave me some instructions, and with the promise of his firm grip on the bike, sent me on my way. After pedaling down the driveway, I looked back, still expecting to see him holding on to the bike. Realizing he was now several yards behind, I panicked and fell. You probably had a similar experience.

Now, what did my father do? Did he say, "Well, obviously you're not cut out for this. Maybe we can try again in a year or so?" Of course not. He shouted, "Great job! You got all the way down the driveway! You just looked away. Now let's see if you can make it down to the corner." He celebrated my efforts, told me what caused my fall, and encouraged me to try again, this time with a new goal. Then he added, "Don't worry. I'm right here if you fall again."

The first fundamental in helping employees learn from their failures is getting them to recognize how and why they failed. But if you instead practice the forgive and forget model, a coaching opportunity will be lost. Or worse, if you criticize or condemn, employee initiative will dwindle. Most importantly, you must guard against the association of failures with risk taking.

Celebration in the face of "failure" allows leaders to forgive and still ensure that employees learn from their mistakes. Using such a strategy, leaders provide employees with a safe forum for them to acknowledge their failures, making the analysis of what went wrong less threatening. They also reward employees publicly for leaving their comfort zones. Celebration as a tactic inoculates employees against the pain of failure while encouraging future risk taking.

Of course, some failures require corrective counseling rather than celebration. Celebrating when a salesperson fails to achieve sales objectives rewards poor performance, sending the message that the goals are meaningless. However, a celebration was in order when, for instance, one of my sales teams lost a bid for a local public institution's coveted banking business. Shortly after the team submitted its proposal under sealed-bid conditions, the institution's purchasing manager telephoned our team leader. This manager called to share confidential information from our competitors' proposals in an effort to create a bidding war—a clear violation of ethics. The team declined the request for a second, lower bid, and the celebration that followed was in recognition of the team's hard work in preparing a competitive proposal, and more importantly, its adherence to the value of integrity.

So how do you celebrate failures? First, guard against embarrassing the employee. The celebration should honor the person's courage in taking the risk, rather than focusing on the unintended results. Honoring the desired behavior encourages future risk taking.

Make celebrating failures a custom—a rite of passage—along the way to becoming a great risk taker. Create a symbolic award that employees can pass on to the next brave person. Set aside a regular moment at staff meetings to present the award. All these steps prevent singling out employees as failures.

If a failure is a team effort, honor the entire team, including the leader.

Use the celebration to debrief what went wrong, as well as what went right. How can we do better next time?

Finally, make it fun. But rather than laughing at the individual, poke fun at any obstacles. Individuals may decide to confess their own blunders—let them.

Many managers receive their opportunities to take risks and meet challenges in the form of assignments. When this happens to you, rise to the challenge. But whether you are a risk taker or a risk seeker, risking personal safety or embarrassment for your values inspires others to follow. Risk taking separates leaders from bureaucrats. It divides those living by their organization's values from those simply offering lip service. It distinguishes those leaders who encourage initiative from those supervisors who are merely exercising control. What type of leader are you?

# Chapter 2

Values-Based Leaders:
## Master both Listening and Speaking

*"The leader's first task is to be the trumpet*
*that sounds a clear sound."*
-Peter Drucker

Almost everyone agrees that communication is critical to effective leadership. In an October 2003 survey conducted by the American Management Association, 84 percent of the respondents listed communication as an important leadership skill—by far the leading answer[1] and, as a result, voted the "top" skill. A Watson Wyatt study from the same year associated effective employee communication with higher company shareholder returns and market value.[2] Yet in a 2002 survey of employee attitudes and opinions, a mere 31 percent rated their companies favorably in communicating to workers.[3]

The way we communicate with our employees impacts how workers understand our messages, and what actions, if any, they take in response. Effective communication goes beyond making certain workers understand our instructions. Values-based leadership must build ongoing "communication relationships," in which people feel included, appreciated, and respected. To achieve these goals, leaders need to use clear language, master the art of storytelling, and listen with their eyes as well as their ears.

## Jargon

The television show *American Idol* gained enormous popularity by showcasing young singers and allowing viewers to vote their favorites toward stardom. After contestants perform on live television, viewers can cast their votes by calling special telephone numbers or by sending text messages. The performer receiving the fewest votes goes home, but all the others return the following week to try again. Each season's winner receives a recording contract and a head start on the road to success.

After each weekly performance, a three-judge panel provides instant feedback to the singers. Randy Jackson, a Grammy Award-winning record producer and former base player for the group Journey, sits on the panel. A music industry veteran, Jackson has mastered his profession's lingo and each contestant, whether male or female, hears a critique that goes something like this:

> "Yeah-uhhh! Yo, yo dude. What's up dawg? How you feelin'? You feelin' all right? Are you chillin'? Listen, man. I've got to give you props. You're doin' your thing and it was dope. I ain't mad."

If you are in the entertainment industry, or a devoted viewer, you probably understand that this performer impressed him. If you are hearing the vernacular for the first time, you are probably confused, to put it mildly.

Thank goodness, the language we use in our professions is easier to understand, right? Or is it? Consider the following compilation of business jargon:

"Let's talk offline after the OD quality circle. With all this synergy, we should tap our knowledge network, benchmark some
competency profiles, and find best practices for establishing
employee engagement through blended learning. I have to go
meet with an ADO in one of our SBUs, but at the end of the
day, it's up to us to find a seamless solution to our disconnect."

Every industry, profession, and organization has its own specialized vocabulary. We use business phrases, buzzwords, abbreviations, and acronyms as verbal shortcuts to streamline communication among colleagues. But rather than improving communication, jargon often hinders it. Organizations believe they are
communicating; but when the words they use lack substance,
leaders leave employees scratching their heads.

## Some people use jargon to deliberately confuse or impress others.

In 2000, a British secretarial recruitment firm surveyed 1,000
office workers. Their study found that one in five are regularly
confused about what their colleagues are saying, but are too em-
barrassed to ask for clarification. More specifically, 40 percent
found the use of jargon in office meetings both irritating and dis-
tracting.[4] Confusion and irritation tend to cause a demoralizing
sense of detachment between the speaker and those who are
listening.

So why do speakers use jargon? Sometimes, they invoke
workplace jargon to impress others, or to establish their membership in an elite faction. Some use jargon to exclude or intentionally confuse others, or to mask their own inexperience or lack of

knowledge. In fact, more than a third of the respondents in the above survey admitted using jargon deliberately—as a means of either demonstrating control or gaining credibility.

If your organization lists open communication among its core values, overusing jargon will destroy your ability to come across as a sincere leader.

## Euphemisms

Candor is central to leadership integrity, but many managers avoid being candid. Telling people difficult news is challenging, so many leaders weasel their way through that challenge by using language intended to soften the blow.

Jargon typically includes euphemisms and substitutes inoffensive expressions for those considered unpleasant. Instead of *You're fired*, we use camouflaging words like *outsourcing, offshoring, downsizing*, or *rightsizing*. Or we use phrases with clinical descriptions of the people whose jobs we're eliminating, like *resource* action or reducing *surplus human capital*. In announcing that DuPont was eliminating 3,500 jobs in April 2004, board chair and CEO Chad Holliday referred to the decision as an effort to "align our resources with market needs and adjust the size of our infrastructure."[5]

The irony with euphemisms is that the action of firing people is still a distasteful one. As a result, the euphemism's softening effect deteriorates over time and the expression becomes just as repulsive as the language it replaces. Does learning that your company is adjusting the size of its infrastructure make you feel any safer than hearing about mass firings?

Credible leaders are sincere and straightforward when delivering news—whether it's good news or bad. However, when leaders sidestep candor with euphemistic jargon, their message comes across as hollow and condescending. Always be direct, honest, and clear. Leave euphemisms to the politically correct. Otherwise, your resulting ineffectiveness as a leader—because of poor communication skills—might prompt your boss to ask you to please *leave to pursue other interests.*

## Ambiguous Expressions

Another reason to avoid jargon is that when employees are unclear about the meaning of jargonistic language, they often distort the message. Consider this example. Many leaders like to proclaim their pursuit of *good people.* So just imagine for a moment that you are responsible for recruiting new employees for your organization. At every company-wide meeting, you stand up and repeat the following request: "If you know anyone looking for a job, please let us know. We're still looking for good people."

Here is what you meant to say with your request: "History shows that existing employees are good sources of job candidate referrals. We like you, and expect that you know other people with your same qualities. You know all about our company and can promote it to your friends. Your friends will value your recommendation. You are all excellent employees, and because we continue to grow, we need more people just like you."

---

## "We're always looking for 'good people.'"

---

How could anyone misconstrue what you said? Remember, our built-in stress response system is always sniffing out danger. Its job is to protect us, so it examines every message we receive to see if it contains a threat. Therefore, employees might subconsciously misinterpret your message. *They're still looking for good people. That must mean they haven't found any yet. That must mean they don't like me. I wonder if they're going to replace me with someone they like better.*

A phrase as seemingly harmless as *good people* is open to more than one interpretation and can cause unintended anxiety. In this real-life example, employees wasted time worrying. This negatively impacted productivity and left senior management struggling to understand why employees were reluctant to refer their friends or relatives. Make sure your employees interpret your message correctly. Help them do that by saying what you mean in a clear and jargon-free way.

## Abbreviations and Acronyms

Here's another example of how jargon leads to misunderstanding. A friend once told me about a rather embarrassing incident. After receiving a notice for an Agency Directors' Association event, he made a point of attending. The organization, which goes by its three-letter abbreviation, advertised the meeting as an update on recent ADA activities. My friend, believing he was attending an update on the Americans with Disability Act, sat through half the meeting before realizing his mistake.

But it turns out there are hundreds of current uses for the abbreviation ADA—everything from Assistant District Attorney, to the American Dairy Association, to the Age Discrimination Act. Too often, we take for granted that our audience understands the abbreviations and acronyms we use.

Many organizations use abbreviations for job titles or functions, for departments, for buildings, for computer systems, for forms, and for even the institution itself. If you are new to UCSD, you may want to visit the CLICS and speak with a CRS in ITD about obtaining an IUC to learn how to access IFIS. Fortunately for you, the University of California, San Diego, publishes an online directory to help demystify its many abbreviations.[6]

Some abbreviations are common to all industries. For instance, sit through a human resource meeting and you will hear an abundance of compliance initialisms and acronyms. Initialism refers to abbreviations pronounced as a series of letters, like FLSA (Fair Labor Standards Act) and FMLA (Family and Medical Leave Act). Acronyms are words formed by the initials or parts of a name, like HIPAA for the Health Insurance Portability and Accountability Act (pronounced "Hip-ahh"), ERISA for the Employee Retirement Income Security Act (pronounced "Err-riss-ah"), and OSHA for the Occupational Safety and Health Administration (pronounced "Ohh-shah"). All are important, as it's conceivable that misunderstanding the identity of any one could lead to substantial fines for your company.

Avoid confusion in communication: spell out your message for listeners.

## MBA-Speak

What makes the problem of jargon chronic is that, every year, new words and catchphrases enter our business vocabulary. Some become permanent additions to our language; others fade away. Although you might still be undergoing a *paradigm shift*, when was the last time you had to *interface* with anyone?

## Jargon overuse might make listeners think you're a fraud.

Many leaders are quick to incorporate the latest business lingo into their oral and written communications. Suddenly, we must pick the *low-hanging fruit,* participate in *global thinking,* and consider our *stakeholders.*

But using the latest jargon to make an impression can backfire. Language that is used solely to impress may instead impress listeners with the speaker's lack of any real knowledge, and reveal a vain attempt to hide behind a wall of words. As the office worker study indicated, that can undermine credibility, since 10 percent of all respondents dismissed speakers using jargon as both pretentious and untrustworthy.

If you are looking for a *best practice* that prevents a *disconnect* between you and your listeners, please, stop *thinking outside the box!*

Why is jargon prevalent among business leaders? Because experts tell us to hide our emotions, and jargon allows us to remove all trace of emotion from our messages. Instead, we focus on the facts and figures, the impersonal numbers on a profit and loss statement. It's cleaner and easier to recite data. Although that information may provide assurances that the company is doing well, or help distinguish the speaker as a knowledgeable expert, it is lacking in one all-important thing: *it fails to inspire.*

When relaying information to employees, studies show that it is critical for leaders to communicate to their listeners' emotions as well as their intellect. The lack of emotional communication is the primary reason jargon is so ineffective as a source of inspiration.

## The Jargon Jungle

Let's examine some popular jargon, paying close attention to how it shades the truth while hiding its real message in, well, jargon. When conducting *The Leading from the Heart Workshop,* I ask participants to share jargon used in their workplaces. Here is a list

of the most commonly mentioned phrases, buzzwords, and abbreviations. How many do you recognize from your office?

AT THE END OF THE DAY: Indicates that you will have
to live with the consequences associated with your actions ("At the end of the day, it's your job at stake.").

BALL PARK FIGURE: An estimated number or price used
for discussion purposes. One of several baseball jargon
phrases (see: Hit It Out of the Park, Knocking the
Cover Off It, and Step Up to the Plate).

BEST PRACTICES: Processes employed by other organizations perceived as the best; in other words, better than
the way *you* are doing it.

BEST-IN-CLASS: Those organizations from whom you
learn Best Practices.

BUSINESS CASE: A projection of what an idea will produce
in new revenues or cost savings: as in, "You can only
have a raise if you can make a business case for it."

BUY-IN: Someone else's agreeing that your idea or project
has value; neglect their buy-in, and they will hinder
your efforts.

CARPET VS. CONCRETE: The relationship between management (administrators working in carpeted offices)
and labor (plant workers doing their assembly line
jobs standing on concrete floors).

CONSTRUCTIVE CONFRONTATION: Sanctioned arguing and battling over ideas; initiated to encourage
innovation.

CORE COMPETENCIES: What an organization or a person does best. Companies like to brag about "exploiting" core competencies.

CORPORATE CULTURE: Traditional behavior at a company; corporate culture is sometimes used to justify bad conduct ("It's just our corporate culture to expect new hires to work seventy-five hours per week.").

DISCONNECT: A disparity or misunderstanding between two parties ("There was a disconnect between what we asked for and what Production created.")

DOG AND PONY SHOW: A presentation to a prospective buyer, complete with slides, handouts, graphs, and testimonials.

DRILL DOWN: Delving into the details of an issue. Requiring further drilling down into the data can conveniently delay making a decision.

FORTY-THOUSAND FEET: Distance from which you should view new ideas in order to see the "big picture."

FRONTLOADED REDUCTIONS: Laying off the largest percentage of people in the early stages of the employee reduction process.

FUZZY MATH: Formerly called "fudging the numbers." When you really need two plus two to equal five, just "round up" from four.

GAINSHARING: Like profit sharing, in that employees share in the company's earnings. But rather than tying incentives to the earnings of the entire company, it rewards workers based on the performance of their individual plants or locations. Beware the term "no pain, no gain."

GLOBAL SOURCING: Purchasing goods for all divisions, anywhere in the world, from a single vendor.

GOOD PEOPLE: The class of employees you would like to recruit. "We're always looking for good people"—as opposed to the "bad people" we apparently employ right now.

**HIT IT OUT OF THE PARK:** A significant sales victory or other major success; a home run.

**HUMAN CAPITAL:** Once called human resources, a.k.a. employees.

**INSOURCING:** Using internal staff members to perform functions once provided by outside vendors. In other words, you don't have enough to do.

**JETTISON EMPLOYEES:** Firing employees as if they were so much unneeded rocket fuel.

**JOB READY:** A prospective employee possessing all the skills required for the job. Actually, this is secret terminology used by HR directors to refer to older and more experienced workers.

**JUST-IN-TIME:** Originally used to describe an inventory-reduction system in which suppliers deliver manufacturing parts as close to production time as possible. You can now use this phrase to explain procrastination at all levels.

**KNOCKING THE COVER OFF IT:** Reaching your target goals so often that the rawhide on the baseball is falling apart (sports-related jargon never seems to disappear).

**LOW-HANGING FRUIT:** Easy-to-pluck targets, such as willing or unsuspecting buyers.

**MANAGEMENT BY WALKING AROUND (MBWA):** Literally refers to managers walking around, visiting work areas, and keeping informed about what's happening.

**MERITOCRACY:** A group of leaders selected because of some individual capability or achievement. Easily tailored to exclude anyone you don't want to include.

OUTSOURCING: Using services provided by external vendors to replace functions once performed by company employees; includes everything from housekeeping services to payroll preparation.

PARADIGM SHIFT: Any change in a generally accepted viewpoint; also occurs every time a new business book reaches the top of the *New York Times* bestsellers list.

QUALITY CIRCLE: A small group of employees from the same work area or job function that meets regularly to resolve problems affecting them. Think: "bitch session."

RIGHTSIZING: Firing employees by invoking the dubious assumption that overstaffing has occurred all along.

RUN IT UP THE FLAGPOLE (AND SEE HOW IT FLIES): Try it!

SEAMLESS DELIVERY: Completing a process without errors or delays or, if that's impossible, making sure the complaints either don't reach or don't bother senior management.

SIX SIGMA: A statistical program used to measure a process in terms of defects. Sigma represents a standard deviation. At six sigma, which experts consider "near perfection," there are only 3.4 defects per million opportunities.

STAKEHOLDER: A person with a stake in the company's financial well-being, including everyone from employees to investors.

STEP UP TO THE PLATE: Come forward and produce results (more baseball jargon).

SURPLUSED: Another not-so-polite way to say firing people; in other words, we can afford to get rid of our surpluses.

SYNERGY: Cooperative interaction among groups—especially among the acquired subsidiaries or merged parts of a corporation—that creates an enhanced combined effect. Often, this is mere wishful thinking, or another example of euphemistic language.

TLA: Jargon for Three-Letter Acronyms that are themselves jargon for other things. Although most are initialisms rather than acronyms, their use may leave you with FAQ (frequently asked questions).

TALK OFFLINE: A conversation held after a meeting. You can use this phrase in conference calls to save everyone else from hearing your meaningless discussion ("Let's you and I talk offline about that issue.").

WORK-IN-PROCESS: In accounting terms, it means goods in various stages of manufacturing. In HR jargon, it refers to employees who show potential, but have yet to meet expectations.

## Stories

We now know that we need to connect on an emotional level when communicating with our employees, so let's look at the best way to make that emotional connection. Briefly imagine how hard it is to sell a product or service your customers think is overpriced. While many salespeople are great lead generators, wonderful at distinguishing their product from the competition's, and then masterfully asking for the sale, they wilt when faced with the question, "How much?" Afraid to forfeit sales because of their high asking price, they extend discounts up front, or accept counteroffers without even *trying* to negotiate. As a leader, how can you help your salespeople overcome this understandable tendency?

One way to do it is by reiterating the goal of increasing sales and profits for the company. Make certain every salesperson understands that stockholders are counting on more double-digit growth, same as last year. Another option is to distribute reports listing those salespeople with low profit margins, and threaten to replace them with salespeople who are more aggressive. I have witnessed both approaches and neither of them work. The salespeople already know that profit margins are important, and they are undoubtedly sensing their own sales weakness.

But there is a third option. When bankers on my sales staff faced this challenge, I told them this story:

Hugh McKenna worked in men's clothing for a department store at our local mall, and he sold me suits for years before passing away. In the process, Hugh taught me more about sales than I learned anywhere—or from anyone—else. For example, one day when I was shopping for a tie, he showed me how important it is to know your customers. I was trying to describe to Hugh the suit I wanted to match it with when he excused himself. A moment later, he returned with a notebook containing a single page for each of his many loyal customers. Attached to the page with my name at the top were swatches from every suit Hugh ever sold me. That day, I walked out of the store with not one but several new ties.

A few years ago, another department store opened at the mall. As part of its grand opening sale, the new store advertised a 25 percent discount on my favorite suit brand. My wife Vicky and I were curious to see the store and stopped in during the sale. I spotted a suit I really liked. I told Vicky, "I'd rather buy this from Hugh. I bet if I go see him, he'll match the sale price." So we abandoned the new establishment and set out across the mall to see Hugh.

Hugh was working that day and he welcomed us in his usual warm fashion. I located the identical suit in my size and Hugh helped me on with the jacket. I told Hugh about seeing the suit at the new store and apprised him of the sale. I asked if he would match the sale price. To my surprise, he said no.

Hugh explained his store's policy against matching the sale prices of competitors. Then he did the unthinkable: he encouraged me to take advantage of the rival's sale. Discerning that I felt both greedy and disloyal, Hugh reminded me that a 25 percent discount was significant. So, with his blessing, we left Hugh holding the suit and hiked back across the mall.

Back at the grand opening, I tried on the suit. Like most people, I have an imperfect build; in fact, I am a long way from perfect. My right leg is slightly longer than my left, and my left arm is slightly longer than my right. My top half is also narrower than the bottom half of my torso. It has always taken a gifted team of specialists, armed with chalk, pin cushions, and shoulder pads, to alter a suit to fit me, and I was accustomed to Hugh's careful supervision of the process. So I was amazed when a salesclerk at the new store glanced at the unaltered suit hanging like a gunny sack from my very individual frame and pronounced it a "Perfect fit!"

"You need to understand," I said, and launched into my laundry list of things that I needed modified.

"Nonsense," said the clerk. "This suit fits perfectly. We'll just hem the pant legs and you're all set." It was only after my continued protests that he acquiesced and summoned the tailor. With considerably less reluctance, he produced the alteration price list.

I always look forward to wearing a new suit. There's something exhilarating about walking around in a fresh outfit, especially when it fits well. At that moment, staring at myself uncomfortably in the fitting room mirror while waiting for the tailor, I had little doubt that this alteration experience would completely deprive me of that wonderful feeling of new-suit exhilaration.

I told the salesperson I needed more time to think about the purchase. I changed back into my own clothes and, once again, Vicky and I trekked back to Hugh's store.

To this day, I can remember that moment: There was Hugh standing by the cash register, a big smile lighting up his face. Hanging on a hook behind him was my suit. "I knew you'd come back," he said.

What's the moral of this story? For my bankers, the lesson was that price and value may be dramatically different, but they are directly related. Hugh understood the importance of adding value to the goods and services he sold. When they perceive value—like Hugh's knowledge of my past purchases and special fitting needs—customers will gladly pay more. But when value is missing, price is the only distinction and then the lowest price always wins. Hugh worked hard to add value, so he was comfortable asking full price.

But the moral of the story for leaders is that stories are the perfect way to make an emotional connection when communicating to your employees.

Researchers have long wondered how we store and retrieve the overwhelming amounts of information received continually in the synapses of our brains. Of specific interest is why we retain certain information but discard the rest. Although it seems logical for our brains to store information by topic, research indicates we actually warehouse and look information up by context; in other words, the stories surrounding the data help us remember the information.

---

# Leaders must communicate to both the emotional and the intellectual sides of a listener's brain.

---

That's why establishing an emotional connection with your listeners is important. And stories like the one above help create the context listeners need to remember your message. A story lets each listener put the message it conveys into a personal context, allowing him or her to absorb the facts in a personally meaning-ful—and hence memorable—way.

But despite the research on the power of stories to provide a memorable context for information retrieval, managers continue to believe that giving feedback is the most effective method of teaching the desired workplace behavior. As a result, employees simply reject most leadership communication.

Feedback often comes across as negative; even constructively delivered feedback is discouraging when it deals with mistakes, shortfalls, or problems. Stories are positive because they recount prior successes and allow listeners to focus on a positive future, rather than dwelling on past mistakes.

For example, we know that successful people tend to reject negative feedback. This is because all of us are more likely to ac-cept feedback if it's consistent with our own positive self images, and negative feedback is inconsistent with how we view ourselves. But since successful people welcome ideas aimed at helping them achieve their goals, they will eagerly listen to stories about other successful people.

On the other hand, whether good or bad, and whether we view ourselves as successful or not, we tend to take feedback personally. In theory, constructive feedback focuses on performance, rather than the individual doing the performing. But since we tend to associate our identity with our work, we inevitably take all feedback to heart. The wonderful thing about stories is that, as they are always about someone else, taking personal offense is impossible.

## When to Tell Stories

Leaders can use stories to promote policies, encourage behavior consistent with the organization's values, or in those situations where they would normally give feedback. When trying to get salespeople to stop leading with discounted pricing, you could humiliate them in front of their peers—or you could tell them about Hugh McKenna.

---

## "I don't want $15—I want my garden hose back."
### Franklin D. Roosevelt

---

Stories are helpful tools for selling your ideas to others. Politicians have long used stories to generate support for their agendas. As Great Britain struggled to defend itself during World War II, its capability to purchase needed arms and materials rapidly diminished. President Franklin D. Roosevelt, determined to find a publicly acceptable way for the United States to help underwrite an Allied victory over Germany, proposed an idea called Lend-

Lease: the United States would buy new weapons—the same weapons Great Britain needed—and lend those items to the British government until the war ended. Then, Great Britain would simply return or replace the weapons. During a press conference held on December 17, 1940, Roosevelt outlined his idea, using a story to make it easier to understand.

> "Well, let me give you an illustration: Suppose my neighbor's home catches fire, and I have a length of garden hose 400 or 500 feet away. If he can take my garden hose and connect it up with his hydrant, I may help him to put out his fire. Now, what do I do? I don't say to him before that operation, 'Neighbor, my garden hose cost me $15; you have to pay me $15 for it.' What is the transaction that goes on? I don't want $15—I want my garden hose back after the fire is over. All right. If it goes through the fire all right, intact, without any damage to it, he gives it back to me and thanks me very much for the use of it. But suppose it gets smashed up—holes in it—during the fire; we don't have to have too much formality about it, but I say to him, 'I was glad to lend you that hose; I see I can't use it any more, it's all smashed up.' He says, 'How many feet of it were there?' I tell him, 'There were 150 feet of it.' He says, 'All right, I will replace it.' Now, if I get a nice garden hose back, I am in pretty good shape."[7]

Roosevelt's story helped him sell the Lend-Lease idea to the American public and, with the public on his side, convince Congress to send war materials to an embattled Britain.

Values-based leaders use stories to illustrate the organization's values. Stories that honor employees for demonstrating those values in remarkable ways are especially effective. Here's an example:

Rachel Shelton worked in my area of our bank selling credit card merchant processing services. Her office was on the sixth floor of our local headquarters. One Friday around noon, on the third of the month, Rachel went to our ground floor branch on her lunch hour to conduct some personal banking. Fridays are the busiest days of the week at banks. Lunch hours are the busiest times of day. The third business day of each month is the busiest day of the month, because government payments arrive by mail and recipients go to their bank to cash their checks. If Rachel was in a hurry, her timing was lousy.

While standing in a very long line, Rachel learned about our bank's newest promotion for home equity loans. All over this branch, brightly colored advertisements encouraged customers to "Ask about Our Home Equity Loan Rates." There were posters on the walls, signs hanging from the ceiling, tent cards on the counters.

After a wait that exhausted most of her lunch hour, Rachel had finally arrived at the front of the maze-like line. Watching for a signal from the next available teller, she overheard a customer's conversation with another bank employee. Apparently this customer had also noticed the signs, for when she completed her transaction, she asked the teller, "What *are* your home equity loan rates?"

"I don't know," replied the teller shamelessly.

Noticeably puzzled, the customer turned and left. The teller nodded to Rachel, indicating she could now approach the window. At last, Rachel's turn had arrived.

But Rachel ignored the teller's gesture. Instead, she left the line and chased after the customer. Catching up to her outside, Rachel admitted home equity loans were out-side her area of expertise at our bank, but she took the woman's name and number and promised to call her with the rates.

Thanks to Rachel, the woman returned to the bank later that afternoon to apply for a loan. Rachel's personal commitment had turned a customer service misstep into a completed sale.

Rachel's behavior characterized our bank's value of providing excellent customer service. This story served as an example of out-standing customer service—and held Rachel up as a model for other employees to follow.

According to Aristotle, "The soul never thinks without an image."[8] Stories help paint a mental image. So watch for stories that illustrate the behavior you value. Highly effective stories in-volve real people in your organization. For instance, a story re-counting customer service heroism featuring someone like Ra-chel—in other words, someone just like them—helps employees visualize what excellent service looks like, so they can imagine themselves responding the same way.

## How to Tell a Story

Of course, having a great story is only effective when you possess good storytelling skills. Too many people would tell Rachel's story in this lackluster manner:

> One time, this woman working for the bank was in the teller line. She overheard a customer ask a teller what the bank's equity loan rates were. The teller said she didn't know, so the employee chased the woman down and got her phone number. Later she called the customer with the rates and made the sale.

Although the version above covers the story's highlights, it hardly holds the listener's attention. The good news is, you can sharpen your storytelling by mastering some simple steps.

---

# State the facts, and then follow up with a story. Let emotions have the final say.

---

First, give your stories titles, such as "The Day Rachel Defined Customer Service" or "Ask Rachel about Our Equity Loan Rates." Titles help make your stories memorable.

When appropriate, name the people involved. Rachel's story praises her for extraordinary effort, so using her name is fine. Otherwise, use only a first name or assign an alias to protect the person's privacy. For instance, if telling about a patient benefiting from the special efforts provided by a healthcare worker, you can say, "A patient I'll call Robert…"

Give details when describing a sequence of events. Explain how Rachel found herself in such a long line, how she occupied herself reading the promotional signs around her, and how she finally made her way to the front of the line. This engages the attention of listeners as they picture themselves suffering in the slowly moving line and makes Rachel's sacrifice all the more remarkable.

Use descriptive language. Describe the busy bank branch filled with social security recipients and the brightly colored rate boards. Relay how Rachel hurried after the customer, catching up to her outside. All this helps form individual images for listeners so they can mentally store the information by context.

Make clear throughout your story which values you are reinforcing. All but one of the bank's employees enjoyed hearing the story describing Rachel's efforts. However, the story is about providing excellent customer service, rather than pointing out how one employee was unaware of the current rates.

Finally, remember that communication is most effective when you speak to both the intellectual and emotional areas of your listener's mind. State the facts first for the intellectual area, then tell the supporting story for the emotional area. But always let the emotional part of the brain have the last word.

To recapitulate: The best way to inspire workers is to engage their emotions, and a direct route to their emotions is through a story. So toss away the spreadsheets and PowerPoint presentations. Tell a good, dramatically satisfying story instead!

## Listening Illusions

Are you a good listener? Ignore that question. Because the ultimate judge of your listening behavior is the person who is doing the talking.

Values-based leadership is about caring, and one of the best ways to show you care is to listen when others speak. If you are going to help workers see the link between their values and those of the organization, you will first need to hear their expressed interests, needs, and concerns.

What's the best way to do that? One trendy communication model instructs leaders to listen actively. In other words, stay focused and show involvement in the conversation by paraphrasing what you hear and repeating key points back to the speaker. *"Let me see if I understand you correctly. You're feeling pressure to complete the project on time?"* If your goal is to annoy people with patronizing interruptions mirroring everything they say, active listening is certainly the way to go. But listening is more than *looking* as if you are interested. It is actually *being* interested.

I have noticed that business leaders often nurture four illusions that frustrate their efforts to listen. Before you can master listening, you must rid yourself of the following illusions.

*1. Leaders believe that, in every instance, they understand their listening role.* When employees initiate conversations, they expect you to fill one of two listening roles: advisor or sounding board. Those soliciting advice want an expert to diagnose their problems and suggest solutions. They may need to draw on your technical knowledge and experience. In short, they are depending on you for answers.

On the other hand, some workers simply crave a confidant with whom they can share their success, or their unhappiness, or their apprehension. Maybe they've already resolved their problems and are searching for confirmation that their solutions are sound. Perhaps they just want to voice their opinions and go on record as for or against the latest company mandate. Rather than advice, they just want someone to listen.

## What's your listening role?

To listen effectively, you must understand your appointed role, the role your employee is asking you to fill, without explicitly saying so. Your unsolicited advice will almost certainly irritate a ranting person. Likewise, when someone asks you to clarify expectations, they might get impatient when you respond with a sympathetic, "Go on, I'm listening." So how are you to know your role?

Situations often dictate it. Perhaps a staff member expresses concern about completing an assignment. If a deadline is looming, the employee probably wants your immediate input. However, if the target date is weeks away, the worker is probably seeking reassurance and your continued confidence.

There are times when an employee wants a listener but needs an advisor. Let's say someone new to supervising reports a setback in getting through to a worker. She would like to save the employee and has some ideas. You vow to yourself to listen and permit her to arrive at her own solution. But it turns out the setback was a criminal act; the employee stole from the company and termination is the only option. In times where there is only one correct answer, you are obliged to provide proper guidance.

Some employees may bluntly tell you to shut up and listen. Others will scoff at your advice, an indicator that they want a listener rather than an expert. But when all else fails, ask. Determine your role by inquiring, "Are you here for my expertise, or my shoulder?"

Good listeners understand the roles employees ask them to fill.

*2. Leaders believe speaking and listening are separate activities.* In other words, leaders often fail to pay attention to how their listeners are reacting to what they are saying. We speak and assume our employees agree. But do they? If only they would give us a sign that they comprehend our instructions, concur with our opinions, or share our concerns.

In fact, we often hear more clearly with our eyes than with our ears. Our employees' body language provides built-in indicators and warning signs that clearly display their real response to our message. Facial expressions, eye contact, hand gestures, and posture all provide clues to how employees are construing what we're saying.

Learning to interpret the basic signals is easy, because nonverbal communication centers on the combination of two key body positions: forward or back, and open or closed. The combinations indicate one of four listener classes[9]:

*Engaged* listeners lean forward in an open position. Indications of openness include placing their hands flat on the table, putting down their pens, or closing their newspapers. Engaged listeners stand with their legs apart and weight on their toes, and sit with their legs uncrossed and their feet under their chairs. They are interested in, and largely accept, what you are saying. This is the best time to make assignments, ask for volunteers, or negotiate agreements.

*Thoughtful* listeners' bodies are open and back, leaning away from the speaker. They might tilt their heads, nod, or blink often. When they look away, it is likely upward and to the right. They may chew their pens, glasses, or fingernails. Thoughtful listeners are interested and receptive to your message, but are not yet in total agreement. Pressuring for commitments or trying to strike an accord will only make them defensive. They need more information and persuasion, and time to think. Provide a few more facts, and then stop talking.

*Combative* listeners are paying attention, but they reject what you are saying. Their bodies are in the forward and closed position. They are probably showing aggression by tapping their fingers or toes, pointing, or clenching their fists. They might stand with their hands on their hips, or shift frequently in their seats. They will look down and to the left. Focus on your message; avoid arguing with them or contradicting any points they may make, because that could lead to anger. Try to steer them toward thoughtfulness by asking that they give the idea some thought.

*Absent* listeners are bored and—as indicated by their closed and back position—they have completely discarded your message. They are probably staring into space, doodling, or checking e-mail. Planning their escape, they may actually begin closing their books, buttoning their coats, or standing up to leave. Your only avenue is to change the subject and try to rekindle some interest.

Although understanding the fundamentals of nonverbal communication is simple, mastering interpretation is complex because the signals are often unreliable.

Since conventional body language is well known, employees often try to send the nonverbal messages they think you want, or to hide the meanings you presume. For example, we expect people who are lying to squirm or avoid eye contact. However, these people know this and can intentionally inhibit fidgeting or force eye contact. In addition, squirming and looking away are symptoms of many emotions, including nervousness, anticipation, anger, or fear. The assumption that a nervous person is lying is an unreliable interpretation of nonverbal communication.

Smiling is another frequently misread gesture. We tend to regard smiling people as happy, or sense that they like us or agree with our message. Although people do signal happiness through smiling, smiles also express fear, contempt, or misery. Smiles can also mask true feelings; workers criticized for wearing their emotions on their sleeve may force themselves to smile regardless of what they are really feeling.

Research shows that most people are unable to hide their emotions. However, although body language conveys important hints about what our employees are thinking, much of our understanding is intuitive and often erroneous. So, should we continue to look for nonverbal signals from our employees? Absolutely. Since we know the best way to inspire workers is to connect with their emotions, the clues displayed in their body language can help us gauge our success.

Of course, you must pay attention. When you speak, watch for the nonverbal signs of what's going on inside your listeners' heads.

**3. Leaders believe they have uncommon gifts for completing several other tasks while they listen.** In their book *Fish! Tales*, Stephen Lundin, John Christensen, and Harry Paul wrote, "You can multi-task with 'stuff,' but you need to 'be there' for people."[10] Leaders who are *there* for their employees are engaged listeners, present in the conversation, giving their full attention to what their workers have to say.

One of my earliest leadership roles was as a manager in a fast-food restaurant. The company, a national chain, pioneered the drive-through window concept. Customers could choose to order their food inside the restaurant, or remain in their cars and shout their selections into an electronic box.

Like most restaurants, we were busiest in the lunch and dinner periods. In slower hours, staffing was minimal. So, in those shorthanded times when walk-in and drive-through customers arrived simultaneously, someone had to wait for service.

Although we preferred to serve everyone quickly, we needed a tiebreaker. Profit—as usual—won. Processing drive-through orders cost less than serving and cleaning up after walk-in-eat-in customers. Therefore, we wanted people to use our drive-through window, and the best way to encourage that behavior was to let walk-in customers watch as drive-through users received priority service.

Verbally communicating our philosophy to customers was unnecessary. Standing and waiting at the counter, observing the favored treatment given to orders blaring over the drive-through loud speaker, walk-in customers got the message: next time, stay in your car!

Your employees can also interpret nonverbal messages. You might assert, "My door is always open." But when an employee stops in to report a concern, where is your attention? Are you concentrating on what the person is saying, or are you checking e-mails while your employee speaks? If you said the latter, maybe your office door is open, but the door to communication is closed.

## What is your body language saying?

You must be an engaged listener. Close the books, put aside all papers, and focus fully on your speaker. Lean forward in an eager and interested position. Unfold your arms and uncross your legs. Show your speaker you value what he or she is saying, are receptive to the idea, or concerned about the problem.

*4. Leaders believe they can expedite the listening process.* The average person speaks at a rate of 125 words per minute. However, most people listen and process information at speeds four or five times faster than that. So they try to drag the speaker along.

Hurried listeners are combative listeners. Are you so anxious that you are unable to sit still? Do you try to push speakers to make their point quickly by saying "yeah, yeah" or "sure, sure," while tapping your fingers or foot, or standing with your hands on your hips? If so, your speaker will know you've formed a hasty opinion and your mind is closed.

Or perhaps you are absent. Are you slumped in your chair, arms crossed, staring into space or down at your desk? Are you doodling or reading e-mail on your computer screen? Have you started putting on your coat? Seeing that, your speaker knows your attention is elsewhere; either you are distracted, or you have simply dismissed his or her opinion as unimportant.

---

## Values-based leaders want to listen, regardless of how much time it takes.

---

Poet and author David Whyte says that leaders must work at conversations. He uses an analogy of a newly married young man who grows frustrated by his wife's unrelenting need to discuss their relationship. Often, their conversations center on the same issues. Why, the man wonders, do they need to talk so much about themselves? If he sat still for one long conversation about their relationship, could he earn a one- or two-year reprieve? Finally, the young man realizes what his wife already knows: conversations *are* the relationship.[11]

It's the same with leadership. Without conversation, leadership would give way to bureaucracy. Therefore, nothing takes priority over talking with and listening to your employees.

## Credibility: The Message Must Be You

As a politician, Ronald Reagan possessed legendary communication skills. He understood the importance of communicating on an emotional level with his audience. In 1980, running against incumbent Jimmy Carter, Reagan asked the American public to consider this question: "Are you better off today than you were four years ago?" The theme caused voters to appraise their lives in relationship to their goals and hopes for a better future, and it won Reagan the election.

In 1984, at age seventy-three, Reagan ran for reelection against former U.S. vice president Walter Mondale. On October 7, 1984, television networks broadcast the election's first debate between the two candidates, live from Louisville, Kentucky. Mondale appeared aggressive and poised, and by all media accounts, triumphed in the debate. Reagan, on the other hand, seemed defensive, nervous, and confused, and struggled to keep up with Mondale's command of specific details and statistics. Despite his massive lead in the poles, the president's age emerged as a dominate campaign issue.

With the next debate scheduled in Kansas City, Missouri, just two weeks later, the White House scrambled to prepare Reagan using mock debates. Administrative staff members fired practice questions at the president and his opponent, budget director David Stockman. Stockman benefited from the written answers, while Reagan continued to struggle with the facts and figures. In his book, *You Are the Message*, media expert Roger Ailes relates how Reagan's campaign team summoned him to avert another disaster.[12] Ailes cancelled the simulated debates and instructed Reagan to stop playing defense and be himself. And he reminded the former actor that his flair for communicating through themes and one-liners got him elected in the first place.

By the time the second debate arrived, Reagan's age was on everyone's mind. When the moderator raised the question, the president went with his instincts. Reagan responded, "I want you to know that I will not make age an issue of this campaign. I am not going to exploit for political purposes my opponent's youth and inexperience." With that response, delivered with Reagan's trademark timing, inflection, facial expression, and body language, he erased the public's fear about his mental sharpness and permanently put the age question to rest.

As a credible leader, you must be sincere and straightforward in the ways you communicate. In other words, you must speak with a single voice, so make sure the voice you use is your own.

## How Employees Listen

An exercise in my workshops highlights how people mentally store information by category. Immediately before breaking for lunch, I instruct participants to set aside pens and pencils and listen as I read a list of ten objects. Their assignment is to memorize the list. The objects are:

1. Window
2. Light
3. Grill
4. CD Player
5. Mirror

6. Seat
7. Odometer
8. Floor Mat
9. Gear Shift
10. Trunk Release

After lunch, I ask participants to write down all ten items. Most are unable to remember all ten.

The results illustrate how people retain and recall information. Only after I read the first several objects is it apparent that the list pertains to things found in or on a car. Once participants recognize what the items have in common, they can mentally file objects by category. So when asked to recollect the list an hour later, most participants correctly remember the second half more readily than the first; in other words, they are more apt to remember those items read after they realized the pattern.

As expected, some participants struggle to recall the first few items. But more surprising than what they forget is what they *think* they remember. Many recall objects found in a car, but absent from the original list—such as steering wheels, hubcaps, and headrests—because they are trying to fill the gaps in their memory.

Were those people listening? Of course they were. But as research has shown, people store and retrieve information by context. In their efforts to remember all ten items, workshop participants search their brains by category. Odometers and gear shifts are clearly associated with cars. Windows and lights are generic; heard before the association with cars is established, those objects are harder to categorize and so more difficult to remember.

Now, imagine this workplace scenario. You give an employee her annual performance review covering several topics, including one or two areas needing improvement. In what you consider a positive review, you praise the employee for her work quality and initiative in problem resolution. Then you stress the need for keeping her supervisors informed when problems do occur. Two days later, you overhear the same employee telling a coworker, "I had a bad review. I need to tell my supervisors about problems, and become a better problem solver."

What happened? Instead of mentally grouping "problem resolution" with "things I do well," the employee somehow misfiled that quality under "areas needing improvement." If yours is like most organizations, it links raises to performance reviews; if you are like most reviewers, you give praise first, constructive criticism next, and discuss salary last. So, while you discuss the review with your employee, she sits there wondering about this year's salary increase. Hoping for a large raise, she's disappointed when you finally announce a 3 percent increase. As a result, the employee stores all your comments, including your praise and the lower-than-expected raise, under the category "things I disliked hearing."

Like participants in the car parts exercise, the employee remembers what she thinks she heard. But what she thinks she heard has to do with the context in which she heard it. So in this case, contextual memory backfired. By understanding how employees listen, you can make the contextual nature of memory work to your advantage.

---

# Use your organization's values to help listeners put your messages into the right context.

---

To communicate information to your employees effectively, help them understand each message's proper context. Establish common denominators immediately. Perhaps the employee's raise has little to do with actual work performance; in fact, she would have ordinarily earned a 6 percent increase, but company belt tightening has dictated a 3 percent ceiling. Therefore, separate the two messages. Tell her about the raise today, and schedule a time for next week to go over her review.

Use your organization's values as common denominators to make even unspoken messages clear. One workshop participant recalled assigning a maintenance worker several duties, including changing a light bulb in a building entranceway. On his way to replace the bulb, the worker ignored debris in the hallway. How, wondered the supervisor, could the worker lack the initiative to remove the trash? Is he simply too lazy? That's one possibility. But what if the common denominator in the list of assignments was unclear? What if the final instruction was "be back here by two o'clock?" The employee might interpret the assignments as "things to do in a hurry." Tie in your values by saying, "Here are some assignments that will help us with our mission to have clean, well-maintained buildings," and watch your workers remember the unspoken tasks you want done.

Everything we do as leaders communicates something to our employees. The words we choose set the tone for openness, respect, and trust. The stories we tell determine how employees remember our messages. Whether we're engaged listeners, or absent ones, our listening actions convey as much to employees as what we say. Remember, it's all about our conversations. So master the art of listening and speaking with your employees.

# Chapter 3

Values-Based Leaders:
## Live By the Values They Profess

*"Leadership is a potent combination of
strategy and character. But if you must be
without one, be without the strategy."*
-General Norman Schwarzkopf

Imagine coming across a company—while you are searching for a great employer—with the following values statement:

"We aspire to be known as a company with the highest standards of moral and ethical conduct—working to earn client trust, day in and day out. Our word is our bond."

After reading that, you immediately think, *This is the place!* With so much shameful corporate behavior making the news, you feel lucky to find a company promoting morals, and ethics, and trust.

The above statement-of-values promise actually comes from a real company—from Citigroup, in fact.[1] But as an investigation by New York attorney general Eliot Spitzer's office has recently revealed, simply expressing values in a mission statement doesn't mean all that much in actual practice. The attorney general's probe uncovered scandalous conflicts of interest at Citigroup's Salomon Smith Barney securities firm.[2]

The Spitzer investigation centered around Jack Grubman, formerly the firm's top telecommunications analyst. Grubman had misled investors with unduly optimistic research reports on AT&T. And he had done so in exchange for a personal favor from Citigroup chief executive Sanford Weill, who also just happened to be Grubman's boss.

Here is the background to this story: In the late 1990s, Grubman was preeminent, one of the highest paid research analysts on Wall Street, who earned up to $20 million per year. It was his buy ratings and optimistic research that helped push telecom stock prices upwards, where they reached stratospheric heights.

The other player in this drama, Sandy Weill, was Citigroup's co-CEO and board chair; he was also a member of the AT&T board of directors. Before November 1999, AT&T management had complained to Weill about Grubman's treatment of their company. From 1995 through November 1999, Grubman maintained a neutral rating on AT&T, repeatedly disparaging the company in his analysis and public comments. At an industry trade show in October 1998, Grubman excluded AT&T from a list of telecommunications companies that he predicted would prove important to the future of the industry. AT&T's CEO told Weill that Grubman's behavior made it difficult for his company to do business with Salomon Smith Barney. A few months later, Weill asked Grubman to "take a fresh look" at AT&T.

On October 20, 1999, Weill attended an all-day AT&T board meeting. The board began discussing the option of issuing a tracking stock for its wireless unit and, as it turned out, Salomon Smith Barney would later compete to become a lead under-writer and book runner for this offering.

A few days later, Weill and Grubman spoke by telephone to discuss the status of the latter's "fresh look" at AT&T. They also discussed Grubman's desire to send his twin daughters to the 92nd Street Y, an exclusive New York City preschool. In a memo to Weill sent November 5, 1999, Grubman provided an update on his "fresh-look" analysis of AT&T. He also sought assistance, once again, to shoehorn his children's admission into the 92nd Street Y. In his last paragraph, Grubman wrote: "Anyway, any-thing you could do Sandy would be greatly appreciated. As I mentioned, I will keep you posted on the progress with AT&T which I think is going well."

On November 29, 1999, Grubman upgraded his opinion on AT&T from neutral to buy, a double upgrade in the Salomon Smith Barney rating system.

A few weeks later, Weill called a member of the 92nd Street Y board of directors, explaining he would be "very appreciative" if she would help Grubman. Four months later, in March 2000, the 92nd Street Y finally admitted the Grubman twins. This same Y board member later called Weill and requested a donation. One of three corporate officers who could authorize charitable dona-tions from the Citigroup Foundation, Weill subsequently ar-ranged a $1 million gift to the Y.

After Grubman's upgrade, AT&T selected Salomon Smith Barney as a lead underwriter in its Wireless IPO. It was the largest equity offering ever made in the United States, and Salomon Smith Barney earned $63 million in underwriting fees. Three weeks after the IPO—and two months after the 92nd Street Y had admitted his children—Grubman began to downgrade AT&T again, issuing negative research reports and making critical comments about the company. Downgrading AT&T twice in October 2000, he returned his rating of the company to neutral.

On January 13, 2001, Grubman e-mailed his friend Carol Cutler:

> "You know everyone thinks I upgraded T [AT&T] to get lead for AWE [AT&T Wireless tracker]. Nope. I used Sandy to get my kids into 92nd St Y preschool (which is harder than Harvard) and Sandy needed [the AT&T's CEO's] vote on our board to nuke [John] Reed in showdown. Once coast was clear for both of us (ie Sandy clear victor and my kids confirmed) I went back to my normal negative self on T. [AT&T's CEO] never knew that we both (Sandy and I) played him like a fiddle."[3]

The e-mail alluded to a power struggle between Weill and Citigroup co-CEO John Reed, and the help Weill allegedly requested from board member C. Michael Armstrong in ousting Reed. Not coincidentally, Armstrong was also the CEO of AT&T. Grubman later claimed that he fabricated the story his e-mails crowed about "in an effort to inflate my professional importance." But the fact is that Citigroup's board removed John Reed in February 2000, shortly after Grubman upgraded AT&T's stock.

In the end, Grubman paid a $15 million fine, and the securities industry barred him for life. Although Weill acknowledged intervening to help the Grubman twins with their admission to preschool, he disavowed any connection with either their acceptance by the 92nd Street Y or the million-dollar donation to the Y made by the Citigroup Foundation. Interestingly, in 2003, Salomon Smith Barney changed its name to Citigroup Global Markets.

Morals, and ethics, and trust? You can't help but wonder because, obviously, those values didn't mean a thing.

## The Ethical Environment Problem

Strong organizational values can play a critical role in preventing—and identifying—ethical improprieties. But, as the Citigroup story illustrates, simply printing a list of values in the annual report is not enough. Leaders must demonstrate those values through their actions. If they violate those values, the price of their corruption is high. Enron investors—many of whom were Enron employees who owned company stock through their 401(k) plans—lost $64 billion when investigators discovered the company's off-the-books partnerships, massive debt, and inflated bottom lines. At Arthur Anderson, 26,000 people lost their jobs after prosecutors charged the company with obstructing justice. After facing accusations of artificially boosting revenues, Global Crossing went bankrupt and sold out to a Hong Kong-based firm. "It's as if we have given the CEOs weapons of mass destruction—at least economically," said accounting professor Brian Shapiro at the University of Minnesota. "The companies they run are bigger than ever. When something happens, thousands can lose their jobs—and more people than ever [have money] invested in them. So a few can do a lot of damage."[4]

---

# "There's a hole in the moral ozone and it's getting bigger."
### Michael Josephson[5]

---

Financial ripoffs at companies like Enron, WorldCom, and Tyco involved much more than accounting errors. The indictments contain words like *concealed, conspired, deceived, disregarded, distorted, eluded, evaded, falsified, inflated, justified, manipulated, sidestepped,* and *withheld*—all of which are words that indicate both intention and deliberation. In other words, these were not mere mistakes.

We often assume that lapses in corporate ethics happen because certain bad apples commit improper deeds. Although that's sometimes true, working in wrongful organizations can make ordinarily ethical people go bad. The bad apple theory attributes workplace misbehavior to a minority of morally deficient individuals. However, it's more likely that a rotten *orchard* is actually to blame.

In too many organizations, normally conscientious employees allow unethical behavior to thrive, afraid to blow the whistle for fear of retribution. In what the *Wall Street Journal* called the "biggest accounting scam ever," WorldCom had $11 billion in hidden costs and overstated profits and revenues. The *Report of Investigation by the Special Investigative Committee of the Board of Directors of WorldCom*, states: "Employees who learned about improper corporate adjustments appear to have feared senior management's criticism or even the loss of their jobs. It was common for employees to be denigrated in public about their work."[6] This, despite the company's guiding principle to "create a culture of open and honest communications," where "everyone should feel comfortable to speak his or her mind."[7]

---

# Forty-four percent of employees fail to report transgressions they observe.
### Ethics Resource Center

---

Many recent corporate scandals were detectable, even avoidable, but workers ignored obvious signs of wrongdoing. Why? According to the Ethics Resource Center's *2003 National Business*

*Ethics Survey*, the top reasons employees close their eyes to misconduct include the belief that management will avoid taking action anyway, and a concern about remaining anonymous.[8]

To promote cultures less tolerant of misconduct, organizations must remain consistent in the values simultaneously communicated to employees and demonstrated by leaders. Hewitt Associates managing consultant Larry Tucker says, "Some organizations pay attention to and reinforce their values, but many others do not. Employees really do notice if there are conflicts between the organization's stated values and what they see in practice."[9]

## Feeling Foolish

"Our idea of what good management is has been hijacked," says R. Edward Freeman, director of the Olsson Center for Applied Ethics. "It's deeply embedded in our culture that business is about greedy little scoundrels trying to do one another in. We've got this idea that business means anything goes."[10]

How do employees react to unethical behavior? One Salomon Smith Barney broker said, "Grubman is an absolute disgrace to our firm…I hope many clients sue!" Another wondered, "Why [do] management and our research department continually defend his advice?" Another scolded, "Shame on him, shame on the banking division, shame on the senior management of this firm."[11]

The above stories may be extreme examples, but they indirectly affect all organizations. As Watson Wyatt's Ilene Gochman states, "With fewer than half of employees expressing confidence in senior management, no company has been left untouched by the fallout from recent turmoil in the business environment."[12]

Consistency between an organization's stated values and its leaders' actual behavior is critical to credibility. When there is discrepancy between what leaders say and what they do, employees immediately and rightly recognize those leaders as frauds.

Here's a typical scenario: Soon after they are hired, employees start observing and interpreting the norms of their organization's cultures. They look for mutual expectations—which of their own interests and needs are consistent with the values of their organizations. Once they feel aligned, individuals can start envisioning their own place in supporting their organization's success. But if they instead uncover an imposter company's real values, employees become confused about their roles. They justifiably feel unaligned, lost, and foolish.

## And Then, All Hell Breaks Lose!

Once workers suspect that management has played them, as Grubman said in his e-mail, "like a fiddle," their behavior begins to reflect that of someone who feels betrayed and duped. When they think, accurately or not, that what they want most is now unavailable to them, they withdraw, become defensive and cynical, start gossiping, and begin causing trouble.

At first, many seek refuge by trying to align with someone else in the organization, such as a respected coworker or a high-level authority figure. Some managers in my workshops tell stories about giving instructions to employees and then watching those employees seek affirmation from coworkers, while others complain about workers going over their heads to more senior-ranking managers. In another variation, some workers will align with the corporate culture itself; these employees commonly say, "I love the company, but hate my boss." Finally, in organized workplaces, disenfranchised workers focus only on the values promoted by their unions. But all these symptoms indicate employees who lack trust in, and have turned away from, their immediate supervisors.

Diminishing initiative and creativity are additional warning signals. Disenchanted workers lose interest and just "go through the motions" of working. Unaligned employees perform only what is explicitly assigned; they stop going above and beyond, and produce only when they know someone is watching.

## Show me the meaning.

Without a sense of purpose or a larger cause, money becomes the unaligned worker's sole motivation. Studies show that what employees want—more than money or titles—is to believe that they are working in meaningful jobs. As a result, the "price" for asking employees to compromise their personal values—when a leader's behavior destroys employee passion, say—is that compensation moves to the top of their list of on-the-job aspirations. What choice do we leave them, in that case?

Employees who feel betrayed by a leader's lack of credibility are not only outwardly cynical, they publicly criticize the leader and the organization. Once a leader violates the organization's values, workers view any attempt he or she makes to rebuild their credibility as a cunning effort to deceive them once again.

Eventually, unaligned workers leave, accepting new employment outside the organization.

## One Foot out the Door

In a major study in 2003 by Walker Information, these employee and customer loyalty specialists found that workers are nine times more likely to stay in their jobs when they believe their organizations act with integrity. But when they mistrust their leaders or are ashamed of their organizations, workers are more apt to consider themselves trapped or at risk.[13] Trapped employees have a low commitment to their organization, but stay for fear of earning less, receiving fewer benefits, or being too incompetent to find other employment. High-risk employees have one foot out the door, lack motivation, are reluctant to recommend their employer to others, and are probably actively looking for another job.

The first step to increasing employee loyalty is ensuring employee trust. Therefore, you must demonstrate your organization's values in your character: Does your company value employee initiative? If so, do you personally seek out risks? Remember, employees need constant confirmation that your stated values are in alignment with the organization's and, thus, their own. So when they observe in you leadership behavior that is consistent with those values, they will know you are worthy of their trust.

## Implied Values

In addition to those values listed in a mission statement, organizational cultures often have unwritten but *implied* values.

For example, picture a company that boasts a philosophy of rewarding hard workers, keeping overhead costs low, and consistently earning high profits for shareholders. Imagine a clerical worker who joined the organization right after high school twenty years ago. Well aware of the company's cost-conscious culture—*there's never enough staff*—she's used to feeling overworked. But, with two college-bound children at home, she believes her primary need is job security. In her mind, by endlessly publicizing its profitability and attributing its success to people like her, the company has implied a commitment to take care of her, as long as she continues to work hard.

But what happens when shareholder pressure to increase profits forces the company to lay off employees for the first time in its history? Even though she will keep her job, how will her behavior change? How will she view the organization's values and her role in its success, now?

Consider the scenario of a company with a long tradition of promoting from within, whose manager trainee program has historically been the breeding ground for its future leaders. Picture an ambitious junior executive eager to get ahead, seeing an opportunity to demonstrate his loyalty by working long hours at entry-level compensation. He likes the company's pay-for-performance approach, and he's betting on future rewards. During his two years in the training program, management consistently praises his efforts. For him, the implication is clear: history will repeat itself, and soon.

Then the unexpected occurs. Hoping to generate more sales, management recruits a rainmaker from a competitor by offering this new recruit a coveted supervisory position. The trainee believes the corporation has violated its values by hiring an outside person for a key management position. Just how many more weekends will he continue to sacrifice for a career with this company?

---

## When you leave it up to employees to perceive the values of the company, you force them to draw their own conclusions.

---

Have these organizations shifted their values, or are its employees basing their assessments on the implied values of the cultures? It's hard to say, because we don't know what their values are—we only know what these two employees *think* they are. But when you leave it up to employees to perceive the values of the company, you force them to draw their own conclusions about whether or not their leaders have violated those values. That's why it's so important to state your organization's values clearly, and to live by them everyday.

## The Values the Organization Professes

Starbucks Coffee Company epitomizes the principle that organizations ought to live by the values they profess. One example of this lies in the way the company purchases its coffee. In 2003, when prices of commercial-grade arabica coffee sold in commodity markets for fifty to seventy cents per pound, Starbucks regularly paid negotiated prices averaging a dollar twenty per pound directly to coffee farmers.[14] The practice allows Starbucks to help improve conditions for farmers in coffee-producing communities and maintain long-term customer relationships on which growers can depend.

At Starbucks, the values listed in its mission statement define the company's culture and guide its employees' behavior. According to Starbucks board chair Howard Schultz, "If people relate to the company they work for, if they share an emotional tie to it and buy in to its dreams, they will pour their heart into making it better."[15] The employees, or partners, as Starbucks refers to them, vigorously agree: seventy-eight percent of the company's partners say the company's values provide meaningful direction in their jobs at Starbucks.[16]

Starbucks takes a commitment to its core values to the highest level. Employees are encouraged to hold their leaders accountable by expressing their opinions on whether the organization's practices are consistent with its mission statement. The company's leaders review all concerns, and employees can expect a response.

In addition, the company publishes a *Corporate Social Responsibility Annual Report*, listing initiatives, programs, and activities that demonstrate how Starbucks provides social, environmental, and economic benefits to the communities where its stores are located. And it takes the added step of hiring a certified public accounting firm to verify the report's content.

---

## "One of the most important roles we have as leaders is to imprint these values on each new generation of the company."
### Orin Smith[17]

---

What makes Starbucks unique? Most organizations choose corporate responsibility over social responsibility. For instance, an organization might be interested in protecting the environment, but it sees its primary obligation as making a profit for its stockholders. An organization giving priority to social responsibility might forgo profits in order to protect the environment—or to maintain jobs. Starbucks operates from the position that corporate responsibility encompasses social responsibilities. In other words, being socially responsible should be a central part of your business objectives, rather than something you do only when there's extra money or time.

Says Schultz, the mission statement is "not a trophy that decorates office walls, but an organic body of beliefs and a foundation of guiding principles we hold in common."[18]

Why are organizational values important? Job candidates are more apt to choose an employer for the organizational values it espouses and practices rather than the financial rewards it offers. Those organizations that recognize the role values play in leadership, and that live by the values they profess, will win the war for talent by attracting and retaining the best workers.

## Hiring from Outside the Culture

Successful companies hire people whose values are in alignment with their organizations. That practice is critical when filling leadership positions. But when newly hired leaders demonstrate values different from those professed by the organization, employees might conclude that the company's values have changed.

Let's say a software firm has a stated value of helping employees maintain a balance between their work life and their personal life, and suppose that policy helped the company successfully recruit a family-oriented professional Web site developer in a competitive hiring market. For the past three years, the developer has enjoyed a flexible schedule, allowing her to leave work early for her children's school plays, ballgames, or doctor appointments, and make up the time later on. Then, a new department manager is hired; he believes work ought to come first and is uncomfortable giving employees so much scheduling freedom. Although he has refrained from stating his beliefs verbally, the new manager has implemented a more stringent timekeeping system to better track how his employees use flextime.

Now the developer must wonder. Does the company still believe in a work-life balance? If so, why did they hire this manager?

Then one day the new manager assigns a coveted, high profile project to a less qualified, single, and childless employee. Does the manager assume the employee without a family has more time to devote to the project? Or was the decision made to give the employee an opportunity to gain more experience? How will the developer with the family react? And how will the single developer interpret the manager's expectations? Does management expect him to work longer hours because he lives alone?

I have witnessed situations just like this. Often, affected employees leave the new manager. And, just as frequently, the manager leaves the company after a fairly short stay.

---

## "I'd rather interview 50 people and not hire anyone than hire the wrong person."
### Jeff Bezos[19]

---

In their haste to attract managers, company recruiters might neglect to fully explain their organization's culture. The omission gives the impression that the organization has the same values as a candidate's current or previous employer, or is looking for someone to bring new values to the table.

For their part, leaders must be comfortable with an organization's culture to contribute fully, so companies should very clearly spell out their values and expectations to applicants during the interview process. Only then can a leadership candidate accurately assess if the company's values fit his or her personal needs and ambitions.

## Managing Change

"How do you manage change?" It is a frequently mentioned challenge I hear when conducting my workshops. Fact is—in today's work world—management is all *about* managing change. But I think the underlying question actually is, "How do you get employees to accept change?" A closer look reveals why employees are loath to accept change.

Most major change initiatives fail because senior management ignores the obvious: managers and employees view change differently. Top managers see change as normal and necessary—as something that's required to meet competitive demands or improve productivity. Employees, on the other hand, consider change disruptive and unsettling. But by eliminating the obstacles in employees' minds that cause anxiety, you can clear the path to change.

Employees first need to understand the mechanics—that is, how the change will affect the way they do their jobs. Imagine your organization replacing manual timekeeping with an automated time clock. Initial resistance could simply reflect questions about using the new system. *How do I insert my timecard? What if I forget to punch in one day? Where do I go if I have questions?* Employees must understand how new things work before they can implement a change.

Next, workers need to embrace the change psychologically. So how well you communicate the facts is critical to ensuring their emotional acceptance. They will probably wonder whether the change will increase their workload, or threaten their job security, and they will expect you to have all the answers. But too many organizations announce changes to the entire workforce at once, including front-line supervisors and middle managers. Then, when employees have questions, their direct supervisors are unprepared to provide the answers. If you want to hasten psychological acceptance, wait to announce changes until your managers are equipped to handle employee concerns.

## Nowadays, it's all about change.

Finally, employees wonder if the change reflects a shift in the organization's values. If your organization professes to trust its employees, does installing a time clock indicate the abandonment of that value? The benefits to automating timekeeping might seem obvious, but our self-protective instincts cause us to imagine the worst. Therefore, take the time to explain what's really prompting the change. Of course, when you live by the values you profess every day, employees are less apt to attribute procedural changes to a wholesale discarding of company values.

When you properly teach your employees how to implement a change, remove any emotional concerns they have, and demonstrate that the organization's values are intact, you will be able to drive change effectively. When you prepare your employees for change this way, they will be less likely to resist new approaches—and more likely to put changes into practice quickly. And nowadays, it really *is* all about change.

## Biases

We all have biases. Someone, probably our parents or teachers, instilled them in us during the course of our upbringing. Biases inhibit our impartial judgment and cause us to confuse stereotypes with reality. Furthermore, biases help reinforce stereotypes in our minds when one incident, or the behavior of a single member of a group, leads us to form an opinion about that entire group. When we make assumptions about our employees' values, we miss out on the opportunity to lead effectively.

---

## Our biases may cause us to mistake what employees value most.

---

During *The Leading from the Heart Workshop*, I break participants into small groups and show them pictures of four individuals. By looking at a snapshot of each person, groups must guess the individual's name, age, race, and family status. They must speculate on each person's occupation, educational background, and hobbies. Just from looking at a picture, they must deduce where each person lives and what make of car each drives. In other words, they must typecast the four pictured individuals by studying their appearance in the photographs.

Try as participants might to suppress preconceptions, their stereotypes are quickly exposed. Participants draw on biases implanted by—who else?—their parents, friends, teachers, and the media. Nervous laughter is common as the labels come a bit too easily.

After each group shares the biographies they have invented, they watch a video of the four individuals telling their true stories. The message is clear: their biases are still active in their perceptions and snap judgments.

But the ways participants answer two specific questions in this exercise have significant implications for values-based leadership. The first question is: what was the subject's most significant accomplishment? And the second: what is the subject's biggest aspiration?

Almost all participants answer those questions with career-related responses. For example, most typically assume a professional-appearing woman's greatest achievement was receiving her MBA, and that she aspires to becoming a CEO. They consider a young-looking man with earrings, spiked hair, and a chin puff to be proudest of his high school diploma, and lacking any aspirations at all.

But, on camera, all four subjects describe their real-life achievements and goals in very personal ways. They report their successes in finding a spouse to love, having children, or potty training a two-year-old. Their aspirations are to be good parents and an inspiration to their families, and to give back to their community. Missing is any mention of money, promotions, or a corner office.

The final question in this exercise asks participants to determine how probable it is that they would meet the individuals in the photographs. Most say it is unlikely they will ever meet any of the subjects. In truth, it is doubtful they would want to meet the people they describe in their answers, because those people are the product of their biases. But the people in the video are real. All are interesting, gifted individuals anyone would enjoy getting to know. How many wonderful people do we miss knowing because our biases get in our way?

Values-based leaders confront their personal biases and understand them well. That awareness, in turn, helps prevent biases from influencing their behavior.

## Rehire Your Employees Every Day

If leaders assume that everyone wants the same things—raises, titles, power—they overlook what *really* may inspire their employees. And since stereotypes lead to mistrust, a fixation that employees are only here for the money causes leaders to distrust their workers.

What if you actually ask your employees what they value? In other words, what if you interview them as if you were hiring—or rehiring—them? Suppose you learn that a valued employee's greatest wish, rather than becoming vice president as you assume, is to raise healthy and successful children? What can you, as a leader, do to help that employee accomplish this goal? Can you build flexibility into the work schedule that will accommodate being present for a daughter's dance recital?

You must "rehire" your workers in this way often. Stop multitasking long enough to ask your employees why they want to work here. I guarantee your employees are asking themselves that question, and that their answers will vary at different stages in their lives.

Maybe an employee once hoped to earn a spot on the executive floor; then along came children and a change in priorities. Or maybe the children are now grown, and the employee is ready to resume a climb up the corporate ladder. Without knowing when changes in aspirations take place, you may continue to make erroneous assumptions about what a worker wants.

## Win As Much As You Can

In *The Leading from the Heart Workshop*, participants play a widely used teambuilding game called "Win As Much As You Can." Four teams receive one card with a large "X" and another with a "Y." In each of ten rounds, every team holds up either their X or their Y cards. Teams win or lose money depending on the combination of cards held up by the four teams.

For instance, if one team holds up an X and three teams hold up a Y, the X team wins three dollars and the Y teams each lose a dollar. If all four teams hold up a Y, each team wins a dollar. Teams can communicate with one another in just three rounds. The only stated objective is to "win as much as you can."

The results are consistent and predictable. Rather than working as a single unit to win as a whole, teams compete to beat one another. Why? First, the instructions are purposefully ambiguous, leaving participants uncertain whether the goal is to accumulate money for their individual teams, or for all four teams as a single enterprise. In rounds permitting teams to communicate, participants typically voice disagreement on the game's goal. Although they recognize that everyone wins when all teams hold up a Y, without a clear objective, participants assume it's every team for itself.

The message to leaders seems obvious: make your intentions clear. After all, the better you communicate your goals, the better your chances of getting the desired results.

But there is another message that comes through, as well: we have long linked goal setting to success, but our emphasis on goals is another cause of the competitive—and sometimes unethical—behavior demonstrated during this game.

---

# Goals help us strive for success, but there are correlations between goal setting and unethical behavior.

---

During the communication rounds, groups normally reach consensus on how to proceed. They might all agree to hold up a Y and allow each team to win a dollar. But the game also rewards deceit, with the highest payout going to the team presenting an X while all others are displaying Ys. Inevitably, at least one team violates the agreement, holding up an X in order to win three dollars. *Hey, the goal is to win as much as you can!*

Although goals help us strive for success, they often inspire unethical conduct when workers fear falling short of expectations. Wharton School of Business professor Maurice Schweitzer says there is a strong connection between goal setting and unethical behavior, especially when rewards are involved. In a research paper written by Schweitzer and colleagues Lisa Ordonez and Bambi Douma, the authors write, "We expect people with unmet goals to be more likely to misrepresent their performances than people without specific goals."[20]

I witnessed the nasty side of goal setting firsthand. Recognizing that some workers are able to give more effort than others are, one former employer implemented an incentive plan intended to reward those salespeople who exceeded expectations. Employees who strived to do their best—while maintaining a normal work-life balance—would continue to receive their current salary. But those salespeople willing to apply the extra effort to meet aggressive goals could earn significant bonuses. It began as a program with noble intentions.

About a third of the eligible salespeople earned a bonus during the plan's first quarter. Those workers had significantly surpassed normal sales targets by working harder and longer. Others who continued to excel earned their regular paycheck without having to choose between attending a child's ballgame after work, and staying late to make three more sales calls. It seemed like a successful incentive program.

However, rather than praising those employees who earned a bonus for extraordinary achievements, senior management focused attention on the salespeople with normal results. Why, they wanted to know, did two-thirds of the salespeople fail to merit a bonus? Suddenly, high goals worthy of added financial rewards had become management's minimum expectation. Furthermore, they now viewed the efforts put forth by a third of the sales force, which they initially considered astonishing, as unremarkable. The incentive plan's goals became a yard stick, and management expected every salesperson to measure up—or else.

That's when the cheating began. At first, employees stretched the rules. The plan offered points depending on the type of income produced. Attracting a new customer earned fewer points than selling new services to an existing client. Convincing a current customer to agree to a price increase earned the highest number of points. Some salespeople offered introductory specials to new clients—large fee discounts for the first six months—and earned points for new customers. When the six-month concession expired, those same salespeople claimed points for increasing fees to regular pricing.

Some salespeople established costly services customers never requested. Others increased some customers' previously negotiated fees without warning. Both practices were easy to hide since most clients neglected to request an itemized bill.

Were these bad people, or did the pressure to meet goals encourage their unethical behavior? Without question, the cheating started once participation in the plan stopped being voluntary. Schweitzer and his colleagues believe that individuals who have goals they fail to meet are more apt to act unethically than workers who are simply interested in giving their best. In fact, experiments by the authors proved that people with unmet goals misrepresent their performance more often than people in a give-your-best environment do.

## Choose what you reward carefully.

Schweitzer's group expected to find people with goals tied to personal financial rewards more apt to cheat than those who had general goals. However, because employees "incur psychological costs from admitting goal failure," the authors found that goal setting alone, even without the influence of financial incentives, could cause employees to act unethically.

How can you realize the known benefits of goals without breeding unethical behavior? First, make certain that results are easily and accurately measurable. Incentive plans allowing employees to report their own results are vulnerable to abuse. Next, avoid all-or-nothing reward systems. Schweitzer found that people who fail to reach their goals by a small margin cheat more than people who miss by a large margin. Says Schweitzer, when promising salespeople "if they sell 30 cars over a set period they will get a trip to Hawaii, you should also have something that is pretty good for the person who sells 29."[21] Finally, choose what you reward carefully. Organizations often promote values like teamwork and cooperation, but build compensation plans around individual efforts.

Thanks to stereotypes, we think of used-car salespeople as slick, insurance agents as pushy, politicians as corrupt, personal injury lawyers as greedy, and postal workers as, well, postal. Now, since the onslaught of corporate scandals, we conceive of business leaders as justice-obstructing, massive-debt-hiding, earnings-overstating thieves who use company funds to purchase personal artwork and put on lavish birthday parties for family members. No wonder only half of all employees trust their senior managers, and less than a third are loyal to their organizations. And no wonder establishing trust with your employees is such an uphill battle.

# Chapter 4

Values-Based Leaders:
## Freely Give Away Their Authority

*"Hierarchy is an organization with its
face toward the CEO and its ass
toward the customer."*
-Kjell A. Nordström and Jonas Ridderstråle

Just about every organization has some sort of hierarchical structure. And everyone who works within a hierarchy—the honchos
*and* the subordinates—confronts the challenges created by this
politically welded structural framework placing authority at the
hierarchical top and compliance at the bottom. In fact, in any
hierarchy, employees simply need to look at the latest organizational chart to find out who has the power to determine their pay,
their job assignments, and their future career development.

By its very nature, a top-down hierarchy places multiple restraints on its employees. Shackled by these restraints (some may
even call them chains), employees feel distrusted and, as a result,
feel inspired to withhold their trust in return.

Another feature of organizational hierarchies is that they tend
to foster a one-sided, top-down accountability. Employees must
produce results—though they have little influence on, or author-

ity over, the process for producing those results. On the other hand, management seldom holds itself accountable for living up to its leadership obligations, such things as providing training, coaching, or financial and human resources. Employees who believe they lack control over—or discretion within—their work, fear their success is totally subject to their bosses' whims and demands.

And this is ironic, because being able to unleash your organization's potential requires placing authority in the hands of those people who actually do the work.

What stands in the way of a *pro forma* handover of authority? There is an old managerial perception that a leader's role is to maintain order and control by first inducing compliance with instructions, and then monitoring the way subordinates comply. Now we understand that the best leaders do the opposite: they renounce obedience, instead concentrating on developing the next generation's leaders. Ralph Nader has said that "a basic function of leadership is to produce more leaders, not more followers."[1] And so, to encourage tomorrow's managers, today's leaders must practice giving away their authority—but in the right way.

## Powerlessness

Let me give you an example. A few days before I was to speak to a group of nonprofit organization executive directors, the lecture hall's facility manager telephoned me. Happy to accommodate any special audio/visual needs I might have, the manager promised to send a technician to meet me in the auditorium a half hour before the event.

On the day of the presentation, after showing me where to connect my laptop computer, the technician disappeared into the control room to turn on the projector. By the time she returned, I had the first PowerPoint slide projected on the hall's mammoth screen. But because the angle of the projector was too high, the slide's uppermost portion wrapped onto the ceiling.

The technician looked at the screen, craned her neck to look at the image on the ceiling, and then asked, "Do you need anything else?"

I pointed out the obvious. Her response was anything but obvious: instead of offering to correct the projection angle, she tried to assure me that the audience would forgive the distraction. When I pressed the issue, she finally admitted, "I'm not allowed to adjust the projector without permission."

Only after I insisted we find a person with authority to alter the angle did she speak briefly by telephone with someone who could sanction the adjustment. Armed with "permission," she asked that I assist her in adjusting the projector. I accompanied her into the control booth.

## "How can I get my employees to take initiative?"

Here's where it gets *really* sad. To adjust the angle, she instructed me to lift the back of the projector while she slid a package of copier paper under the rear of the machine. Now the projection angle was too low, so I lifted the projector again and she removed some paper from the package. After a few tries, the angle was finally perfect.

Without more background information, I cannot judge why a technician needs permission for such a trivial operation. Perhaps she dropped the projector on the floor during a previous alteration, or maybe the machine is especially sensitive, and the simplest adjustment could interfere with its performance. But one thing I can say with certainty: that technician feels powerless. So it's highly unlikely that she will ever take an independent step. Her frame of mind is a perfect example of hierarchical restraints—or chains—in their most detrimental form. Nevertheless, leaders often ask me, "How can I get my employees to take initiative?"

Here are some reasons they might resist: When workers sense they lack control over their work, they are less motivated, less productive, and less willing to venture outside their comfort zones. Some attribute their powerlessness to a bureaucracy or an authoritative manager's weakness; others blame their own incompetence. To overcome employee reluctance to take initiative at work, we need to explore the conditions that cause employees to feel powerless more carefully.

## Organizational Causes of Powerlessness

In many organizations, obedience, compliance, and dependency are legislated. In others, culture and tradition dictate conformity. Too many written or implied restrictions create a sense of powerlessness, forcing employees to surrender their initiative to the "chain" of command.

And it's true that when companies transition through major organizational change, such as buyouts or mergers, it is normal to have dramatic fluctuations in goals, rules, and reporting structures. As responsibilities shift, individual departments or divisions—or even entire companies—may perceive a loss of power or political influence. Employees face greater job insecurity while having to accept and acquire new responsibilities and skills.

---

## "The bottleneck is at the top of the bottle."
### Gary Hamel[2]

---

But as I mentioned earlier, bureaucratic environments, by their very nature, are breeding grounds for employee powerlessness. By their reliance on rules, routines, and conventions, bureaucracies encourage dependency and submission. There's little room for initiative or risk taking, and employees closest to the front line are, in any case, excluded from the decision making process. Author and strategist Gary Hamel says that rule makers at a bureaucracy's top typically have the least diversity of experience, the largest investment in the past, and the greatest respect for industry convention. As a result, rules are typically outdated as well as impractical.

Poorly defined reward systems can also make employees feel powerless. Arbitrary salary plans that lack any correlation between performance and pay, leave workers attributing their level of compensation to a supervisor's quirks. How can I get ahead when I work harder, take more initiative, and welcome more responsibility than my coworkers accept, but we all get the same 4 percent annual pay increase regardless? Furthermore, many organizations offer one-size-fits-all incentives that ignore the personal needs and interests of employees. For instance, a five-day cruise for two—a great reward for many—probably creates more hardship than inspiration for an employee with a newborn child at home. What that employee might truly appreciate is a new digital camera for capturing special moments with the baby.

Many other organizational factors limit employee control over their jobs and events at work. Organizations under excessive competitive pressures often set unrealistic goals that employees feel powerless to achieve. Centralized or remote operational resources eliminate any sense of influence over quality, and create confrontational "us vs. them" work atmospheres. Unreliable computer systems and communication networks leave employees feeling stranded. In those environments, teamwork, empowerment, and open communication are nonexistent, and workers view any efforts to profess those values as mere lip service.

# Leadership Style Causes of Powerlessness

Why take initiative if my micromanaging boss tells me in painstaking detail how to do something, or overrides me when I try something on my own? If my negative manager has me convinced I am inept, why should I take on extra work and open myself to extra criticism? And if my boss withholds the big picture from me, how can I see beyond my specific task?

## Micromanagers

A manager was describing a leadership dilemma to me one day. In exchange for a paycheck, the manager explained, he asks only three things of each employee: show up, show up on time, and show up in uniform. With such simple expectations, he wondered, why does he face ongoing absenteeism, tardiness, and dress code violations?

Expecting so little from employees betrays the symptoms of micromanaging. Micromanagers operate from a lack of trust—they distrust their employees—so they feel the need to maintain complete control. As a result, they set modest expectations: come to work, arrive on time, dress appropriately.

A micromanager's expectations often create self-fulfilling prophecy situations, in which employees live up or down to whatever managers expect from them. For example, when the greatest challenge their boss assigns is to dress properly each morning, workers sense a lack of faith—and an expectation of failure—from that supervisor. As a result, employees expect less from themselves. Their performance reflects those low expectations and, not surprisingly, their supervisor's self-fulfilling prophecy comes true.

But how is it possible for employees to sense a microman-ager's low expectations? As a professor of social psychology at Harvard in the 1960s, Robert Rosenthal did extensive research into self-fulfilling prophecies in education.[3] By convincing ele-mentary school teachers that specially designed testing had identi-fied those students about to enter a period of academic and intel-lectual blooming, he was able to manipulate the teachers' expecta-tions for their students. In three classrooms at six different grade levels, Rosenthal randomly selected an average of 20 percent of the students and identified them to teachers as showing unusual potential for intellectual improvement. Eight months later, the arbitrarily selected bloomers had shown significantly greater gains in IQ than other students in the classes.

Certainly, teachers paid special attention to those students Rosenthal had identified as bloomers. But Rosenthal also studied how teachers behaved toward students for whom they had low expectations.[4] Notice the similarities between these teachers and those leaders who expect less from certain workers:

- Teachers seated low-expectation students farther away and sometimes clustered them in groups.

- Teachers paid less attention to low-expectation students in academic situations, calling on them less often to answer questions or to make public demonstrations.

- Teachers allowed low-expectation students less time to an-swer questions, and deprived them of clues and follow-up questions.

- Teachers smiled less often at, and maintained less eye con-tact with, low-expectation students.

- Teachers criticized low-expectation students more fre-quently for incorrect responses.

- Teachers praised low-expectation students less often for successful answers, but applauded them more frequently for marginal or inadequate responses.

- Teachers gave less accurate and less detailed feedback to low-expectation students.

- Teachers demanded less work—and effort—from low-expectation students.

Micromanagers display the very same behaviors toward their employees. They ignore them, smile at them infrequently, spend little time teaching them new skills, withhold company news from them, and demand less of them. And because they lack trust in their employees, they often end up doing the work themselves.

---

## Leaders who consider *themselves* effective are less apt to micromanage and more likely to set high expectations for their employees.

---

If you demonstrate micromanagement tendencies, you might argue that forming expectations is unavoidable. As one manager told me, "I'm not a micromanager, but you have to be careful." She then described allotting an employee two weeks to produce a report for the board of directors. A week later, she asked for a preview. Halfway to the deadline, the employee unveiled a half-completed, albeit on-schedule, report. Rationalizing that the employee was running out of time, the manager took back the project and hurriedly produced the report herself. "You," I told her, "are, in fact, a poster child for micromanagement."

By altering some internal beliefs, you can prevent self-fulfilling prophecies from developing. Surprisingly, it is the expectations micromanagers have for themselves that must change. Leaders who consider themselves highly effective are more apt to view all workers as reachable, teachable, and worthy of attention. Managers who attribute their employees' accomplishments to their own success as leaders will probably help their workers grow. You must believe, regardless of your perceptions of each employee's potential, in your own abilities to teach and inspire.

Freely giving away their authority requires micromanagers to set high expectations for their employees. But more importantly, they must demand greater things of *themselves*.

## Highly Negative Managers

Here's another managerial stumbling block. I was meeting with a friend of a friend, making a sales pitch for my workshop. During our conversation, she confided some of the frustrations she felt in a new leadership role, and half-jokingly described herself as a "bad manager." But as our discussion was nearing a close, she articulated the paradox of many new leaders. "I know," she said, "that it's possible to be a good leader and still have people like me."

I had heard this dichotomy mentioned many times before. In fact, countless management sages advised me during the early days of my corporate career, "Leadership is not a popularity contest. Your employees don't have to like you; they just have to respect you." Accordingly, in my first few management roles I felt a bit spineless when—in my heart—I truly cared what my employees thought of me as a leader, and as a person.

That said, the truth is, being a negative manager came quite easily in my initial leadership positions. Scared to death of failing,

I wanted—or, more accurately, hoped for—perfection from my employees. So I criticized mistakes, denounced setbacks, and ridiculed unconventional suggestions. Far from being a management style, being a negative manager was a symptom of despair.

Then I realized something that justified ignoring the advice of my well-meaning mentors. I remembered my own lack of respect for bosses who I disliked. And a better guiding philosophy for leadership suddenly became clear to me: employees really have to like you *before* they can feel respect for you.

Unfortunately, many managers continue to act as though respect is something they can demand. Sometimes the abuse is extreme. Managers may use deprecating names for employees, yell at workers for disagreeing, threaten people with job loss, single out individuals for humiliation, or even initiate physical contact. Less extreme behavior includes withholding important information, staring, or giving employees the silent treatment.

---

## Abused employees will retaliate— not toward the boss, but against the organization.

---

Because negative managers telegraph their feelings, their conduct causes further harm to their direct reports. Coworkers, who pick up on the manager's behavior, grow suspicious of the abused employees and revise their own opinions about those individuals. Colleagues may then exclude them from project teams, second guess their ideas, mistrust them, and actually dislike them. As a result, interpersonal battles emerge and productivity suffers.

In an article for the *Journal of Applied Psychology*, researchers Kelly Zellars, Bennett Tepper, and Michelle Duffy point out that negative management has serious implications for organizations.[5] Abused workers, striving to preserve some self-esteem, are apt to reciprocate their manager's hostility. But rather than directing their revenge at their supervisor—and risk sparking further hostility from their boss—employees respond by withholding actions that benefit the organization.

In their research, the authors found that abused employees retaliate by refusing to display what academics call *organizational citizenship behavior*. Instead, abused workers seek justice by denying assistance to coworkers, complaining about petty problems, being uncivil to fellow employees, and criticizing the organization in public. Such conduct is damaging to the company, but rarely punishable; therefore, employees consider the behavior a safe way to avenge negative management.

If you work in an organization with frequent changes, intense competition, or unrealistic goals, you may find yourself succumbing to the frustration all these things cause by exhibiting some negative manager traits. And, on rare occasions, you may actually succeed in bullying people to up their level of performance to a certain degree. But in the end, your employees will settle the score by withholding their best efforts.

Values-based leadership allows you the luxury of being effective *without* abusing your workers—and permits them to like you as a result. By proactively demonstrating the organization's values, you will show employees your alliance with their values, while simultaneously validating their positive feelings about you.

## Poor Communicators

In a 2002 workforce survey, Watson Wyatt found that only 49 percent of all employees understand the steps their organizations are taking to reach new business goals.[6] That means half of all workers are unable to see a link between their jobs and their organization's objectives. Watson Wyatt's Ilene Gochman warns, "This is extremely unfortunate because we know that there is tremendous positive impact to the bottom line when employees see strong connections between company goals and their jobs. Many employees aren't seeing that connection."[7]

## How can leaders who fail to portray company objectives expect employees to work together?

Now consider this: getting workers to collaborate when they have different goals or agendas is the top challenge among today's leaders, according to a survey by the American Management Association. Sixty percent of surveyed executives listed getting people to work together as the biggest hurdle they currently face.[8] Taken together, the two surveys reflect the repercussions for leaders who are unable—or unwilling—to communicate their organization's vision.

Maybe you've seen this problem in your organization: management instructs employees in the billing department to not only collect and post receivables, but keep overhead low, as well. In other words, operate with the fewest employees possible and limit overtime by squeezing twelve hours' worth of work into eight-hour shifts. Meanwhile, over in sales, new business acquisition is the aim. *Grow big, grow fast, and grow now!*

Then the two objectives collide. The sales department acquires a large account that generates significant revenue—and a tremendous increase in the number of payments to process. As directed, the billing department has been operating lean and mean; the new business increases volume by 20 percent and brings an already overworked department to its knees. Performance suffers, payments are misapplied, and the new customer is upset.

Sales: "You're not servicing our clients!"

Billing: "Stop bringing in new business when we don't have the necessary resources."

Most leaders recognize that better communication with employees is the key to getting people to work together. In fact, 84 percent of the AMA survey respondents listed communication as the most important skill needed for effective leadership.[9] So what's the problem? Usually, it's that leaders are communicating the wrong message to their employees.

Let's say the organization in our example has a mission to increase shareholder value by providing exceptional service. However, messages from management have an emphasis on numerical results: cut costs; grow now.

The secret to getting workers to understand multiple goals and work together to achieve them is simple: eliminate the separate (and at cross-purposes) goals. If the organization's vision is to increase profits through excellent service, leaders should convey a single message about servicing the customer. When salespeople understand that an unprepared billing department is unable to service new customers, they will bring billing supervisors into the sales process. Informed about potential new business in the pipeline, billing supervisors can plan and staff accordingly. Suddenly, everything works because there is one vision and one goal.

Communicating a common vision requires skills largely neglected in the business world. (In chapter 6 you will learn how to separate yourself from other business leaders by developing those important skills.)

## Why Empowerment?

Values-based leaders recognize that employees are more effective when they can influence how they do their jobs. Today's flatter organizational structures and streamlined workforces have led to increased responsibilities and workloads for many employees. Giving authority to workers on the front lines—who are ultimately accountable for the outcomes of their actions, anyway—is a cornerstone to job enrichment.

Increasingly, employees regard personal control as an important factor in determining job satisfaction. That's especially true for workers from Generation X (born between 1963 and 1977) and Generation Y (1978 to 1984). Employees from those generations probably grew up in households where both parents worked, were divorced, or lived a permissive lifestyle. Therefore, they spent more time alone as children than their parents did, and they are consequently more independent and self-reliant. Better educated, many are resistant to direct supervision and skeptical about hierarchical authority. Clearly, for Generations X and Y, empowerment is a meaningful incentive.

Responsibility can also serve as inspiration in lieu of other rewards. After assuming the role of backroom deposit operations manager following a bank merger, I learned the parent company considered a majority of my new employees overpaid under its salary plan. My first duty was to inform my most highly experienced and knowledgeable staff members about the unlikelihood of future raises. My one good fortune was inheriting an extremely flat department organization structure; there were 110 employees, two assistant department managers, and me. So I offered leadership responsibility to the most qualified—and overcompensated—veterans. I declared each a unit leader, empowered to oversee a small group of employees performing a common function. And it worked; all the individuals to whom I made the offer remained and thrived in their leadership roles. They stayed with the company because I gave them something they craved more than money—influence over their work.

As the research on psychological hardiness indicates, job control plays a major role in reducing the detrimental effects of stress on performance and health. People who believe they can control their environments are better able, and more willing, to adapt to change.

## Who Wouldn't Want Empowerment?

Despite positive results for employees who can exercise control over their work, managers hold four fundamentally flawed beliefs about employee initiative:

*1. Managers assume their employees know, or ought to know, that the organization wants them to take initiative.* Only when you help employees overcome their fears—by creating a safe environment to take risks, where you celebrate failures as milestones of personal growth, and share authority through trust—will your employees understand that you value initiative. Then, and only then, will they respond the way you hope they will.

*2. Managers presume that all employees welcome the freedom to take initiative.* Humans have an innate desire to contribute, but that passion conflicts with our natural instinct to protect ourselves against things we fear—things like rejection, failure, embarrassment, or retaliation. Most people embrace having control over their work, but the perceived emotional danger of empowerment overcomes many others.

Individuals who take failures personally have an exaggerated sense of their own incompetence. They view taking initiative as futile since they expect to fail. They relinquish control because another failure would only confirm their negative self-image. Empowerment puts them in a psychologically threatening position.

*3. Managers conclude that employees who avoid taking initiative are lazy.* Sure, some employees are lazy; for them, empowerment means extra work. But we must avoid mistaking caution for laziness. Some workers are still nursing wounds from prior initiative-taking episodes. Someone empowered them and they took some initiative; then, that person stripped away their power and criticized or humiliated them. *Fool me once, shame on you. Fool me twice, shame on me.*

*4. Managers think they've finished their work once they've given away their authority.* Empowering leaders understand that by giving away authority, they actually increase their own responsibility.

Because the obvious candidates for empowerment are those employees highly skilled at the technical aspects of their jobs, some managers undersell expectations when granting authority to experienced employees. In doing so, they set these employees up to fail, only to exude irritation or disappointment with them at the first sign of trouble. Although dictating step-by-step instructions is unnecessary, you do need to explain objectives, outline timetables, install appropriate checks and balances, and provide all the required resources. Also expect to repeat yourself as many times as employees need to hear your instructions.

Ongoing encouragement is critical for building sustainable self-confidence, so voice confidence in your empowered employees continuously. Too often, managers withhold unpleasant feedback early on because they fear criticism might demolish an empowered employee's enthusiasm. Some bosses, hoping to avoid micromanaging, mistakenly assume employees will ask for help when problems arise. But without constructive feedback, how's a worker to know a problem exists? You have an obligation to get involved quickly when problems arise; by sitting on issues, you deprive employees of your guidance.

You are also obliged to support the employees you've empowered before others call their authority into question. Begin by talking openly about giving away your authority. Make it known to all concerned that you've authorized those employees to act for you and in what capacities. Then make it clear that second-guessing those workers is intolerable. There are few things more frustrating to an empowered employee than confronting colleagues who question, "Who gave you the authority to make this decision?"

Finally, when you give away your authority, resist any urge to take it back.

## Listening to Empowered Employees

Here's another fine point to keep in mind when empowering your employees. When they count on you to fill the advisor listening role, employees are looking to you for answers. As a leader who freely gives away your authority, your challenge is to make sure you are answering the right questions. Otherwise, you might unintentionally strip workers of the very independence you are trying to encourage.

When faced with roadblocks, some workers want you to clear the backed-up traffic for them. However, empowered employees might simply want directions to the nearest resources so they can steer themselves around the roadblocks. When you assume they are looking for a step-by-step roadmap for resolving their issues, you might be taking the fun out of being empowered. More importantly, employees might interpret your rush to intervene as a repossession of the authority you gave them.

Two bad things can happen when you interfere with an employee's problem-solving efforts. First, the employee might stop telling you about impediments and setbacks. That could lead to unnecessary frustration for you both. Second, the employee might spurn your future empowerment efforts. After all, why get excited about having authority when the boss continues to do all the managerial thinking, while at the same time lamenting, *Why won't my employees take initiative?*

Incidentally, this dilemma is a common shortcoming in many corporate mentoring programs. Rather than guiding employees through the problem-solving thought process, these gurus summon up and hand over proven solutions from their past. As a result, employees fail to develop analytical skills, and mentors pass tired solutions on to future generations.

Knowing your listening role is a prerequisite to giving away your authority.

## Disrespectful Employees

Although it may seem far-fetched, the story of a nineteenth-century obstetrician can provide modern-day leaders with a meaningful lesson in dealing with some "disrespectful" employees. In the middle 1800s, women giving birth in public hospitals throughout Europe risked developing the deadly disease puerperal sepsis or, as many referred to it, childbed fever. Doctors had not yet discovered a connection between germs and disease, and mothers were dying at alarming rates. The conventional medical wisdom proclaimed childbed fever as simply not preventable.

Hungarian-born Ignaz Philipp Semmelweis was assistant physician of midwifery at Vienna General Hospital in 1847.[10] The hospital, which served primarily poor and unwed women, had two delivery wards, one staffed by medical students and the other by midwives. Dr. Semmelweis observed that 13 percent of the patients in the medical student ward died from childbed fever, compared with only 2 percent of the patients in the ward attended by midwives. He began to suspect that the students, who practiced surgical techniques by dissecting cadavers, were transmitting the fever as they moved back and forth between performing autopsies and treating patients. When a friend and colleague cut his finger during an autopsy and died soon after from puerperal sepsis, Semmelweis was convinced he had unearthed a correlation between his colleague's death and the patients who contracted the disease after students who were also dissecting cadavers had treated them.

To Semmelweis, the solution was obvious. He instructed students to wash their hands after performing autopsies and before examining patients. The results were dramatic. Mortality rates for the two wards were now comparable. Next, he directed students to wash the medical instruments used in the delivery process. Soon, Semmelweis had virtually eradicated childbed fever from the ward.

Semmelweis was slow to publish his findings, but when he did, mainstream medicine belittled his conclusions. The idea of washing their hands seemed undignified and humiliating to physicians who considered their profession divinely blessed. Also, doctors were unwilling to admit their inadvertent role in causing the deaths of unknown numbers of patients.

> ## "Not all malcontent employees are mavericks, but virtually every maverick is a malcontent."
> Wayne Burkan[11]

Semmelweis openly raged at the stupidity of his peers in the medical community. Despite his attacks, physicians and scholars remained unconvinced. He suffered from insanity brought on by his inability to sway the scientific world. After his death, Louis Pasteur proved him right.

Semmelweis was a nonconformist whose confrontational style overshadowed his good intentions and created disharmony. To Semmelweis, his discovery was so logical—and so beneficial—that he never imagined his findings would threaten his peers. Therefore, the unexpected resistance displayed by his critics frustrated him and caused him to lash out vehemently. The more Semmelweis insisted, the more his peers balked, until the cycle drove him mad.

It is often difficult to distinguish the good malcontents—or mavericks as author Wayne Burkan calls them—from the everyday chronic complainers. As a result, the tendency is to treat all eccentrics as mutineers and, in doing so, we effectively discard our creative thinkers. Managers are quick to dismiss the ideas and concerns of low-ranking or ineloquent employees. The maverick grows frustrated (*it's so obvious*), becomes more vocal, and eventually earns the disrespectful employee label. After resigning, the rebel tells all at the exit interview, but management simply interprets these comments as more whining from a disrespectful employee. *Good riddance!*

If you attribute free thinking to disrespect, your personal biases and preconceptions may result in missed opportunities. Employees who disagree with you, and take the risk of saying so, can introduce new perspectives, raise provocative questions, or bring attention to unforeseen problems. But if you respond with an onslaught of rejection—the aptly named Semmelweis Reflex approach—your employees will in the future refrain from challenging conventional wisdom. Instead, they will fritter away their insights while swapping lunchroom grievances with coworkers.

How should you handle your Semmelweises? Start by ignoring those inner voices and preconceptions that declare every new idea radical; after all, the conflict with your instincts is what makes the suggestion seem unorthodox in the first place. If your mindset makes every outcome a foregone conclusion, your risk takers will stop challenging the status quo and you'll find yourself left with a staff made up of past perpetuators. But questioning your intuition opens you to tremendous opportunities.

Beware the prejudices of prevailing experts. When Semmelweis challenged the long-held belief that childbed fever was unavoidable, the Vienna medical establishment rejected a handwashing prevention proposed by a lowly obstetrician from Hungary. Likewise, the marketing department will probably rebuff a new product idea from someone in your accounting area. Just as giving away your authority is difficult, having an outsider challenge how you do your job may be equally threatening.

---

## Some stand out for what they propose; some for what they oppose.

---

What is the antidote to the Semmelweis Reflex? Help employees to sell their unconventional ideas. Because mavericks consider their theories incredibly obvious, they believe anyone who resists is either foolish or deliberately standing in their way. In fact, a maverick's inability to articulate a good suggestion is often what really gets in the way of its acceptance. The resulting frustration leads to dissident behavior that appears to be disrespectful.

If you are unconvinced an idea has merit, but certain a persistent employee is acting in the organization's best interest, invest resources in helping that individual present an effective argument. Perhaps someone in marketing or sales could assist in creating a proposal. Then you can consider the idea on its intrinsic worth.

Some mavericks stand out for what they propose; others for what they oppose. Writing in the October 2000 edition of *Fast Company*, former U.S. labor secretary Robert Reich proclaimed, "The most hard-core resisters are often found at the most successful companies—because prior successes give them an excuse for resisting, even in the face of mounting evidence that change is required."[12] Again, you must distinguish the overcautious protectors from the people who are simply uncomfortable with change. Treat warnings from resisters the way you would handle any new idea—ignore preconceptions, prevailing wisdom, and communication styles—so you get all the good advice available. Show employees threatened by change that although new procedures, computer systems, and personnel are inevitable, the values that attracted them to your company remain constant.

You don't need to tolerate truly disrespectful employees—those who actually demonstrate a lack of respect toward you. But every organization has people like Semmelweis. Rather than "washing your hands" of yours—learn to cherish them instead.

## Let's Go to the Replay

Everyone makes mistakes; by catching your mistakes early, you limit their negative impact. In 1999, after an eight-year absence, the National Football League reintroduced instant replay to professional football officiating. Thanks to improved technology, coaches can now challenge certain calls made by game referees. Let's say an official rules that a receiver made a spectacular catch resulting in a touchdown. The opposing team's coach, who's convinced that the receiver's right foot was out of bounds, may contest the ruling. Refs then watch slow-motion instant replays, looking for indisputable evidence that the player stepped out of bounds. If the replays show the player's foot over the line, officials reverse the call and negate the touchdown.

In leadership, as in sports, having your decisions second-guessed is unnerving. But people brave enough to disagree with you can put forth new ideas, warn you about unexpected problems, or tell you when you've made a bad call. And since you are a risk seeker with the courage to question bad decisions made by your superiors, you will want to instill that same behavior in those people reporting to you. So, what if you implement an instant replay process for your employees? In other words, give workers a safe way to challenge your calls.

Unless you show workers that you unconditionally welcome their feedback, many will balk at challenging your directives; some might have misgivings about showing disrespect, while others will fear retribution. In football, coaches initiate instant replay challenges by tossing a red flag onto the field. You could give employees flags to drop on your desk whenever they want to question a decision—thereby encouraging participation and providing bashful challengers with a fun, unthreatening way to approach you with concerns.

In the NFL, only specific plays are disputable; for instance, officials can use replays to determine where exactly a runner stepped out of bounds, but pass interference claims are unchallengeable. You should steer clear of setting similar stipulations. Sure, without such limitations employees might question every decision you make. *Why did you give Mary next Friday off when I asked first?* But that's better than having employees wonder what issues are questionable. Besides, if you are truly sincere about getting feedback, you need to hear it all.

There's one other NFL rule to avoid. When officials determine that the original call was correct, the challenging team must forfeit one of their time-outs. You should not assess any penalties when employee challenges are overruled.

One final tip: NFL coaches must initiate challenges before the next play begins; otherwise, the call stands. Your replay system should have a time restriction as well—a three-day limit, for example—to prohibit employees from allowing their issues to fester for too long.

You and NFL officials have a common goal: avoiding mistakes that harm the outcome. But while coaches challenge from the sidelines, you will need feedback from the frontlines. Freely give away your authority by introducing instant replay in your leadership game.

## The Manager as Producer

Sharing your influence and the prestige associated with leadership often requires confronting your insecurities about losing power. And if you are among the growing ranks of business leaders who must both manage others and meet personal production goals, that challenge becomes even greater.

For the most part, people earn their leadership roles by demonstrating other job-related skills. *You're a good salesperson; we're going to make you the sales manager.* However, as demands to reduce costs and operate with fewer employees increase, more managers are taking on dual roles as managers and producers. Now, in this example, the best salesperson has the added duty of overseeing the sales staff.

In their book, *Player Manager*, Philip Augar and Joy Palmer examine how various leaders juggle the simultaneous responsibilities of managing and playing on the team.[13] There's the new manager who tries to do it all; the manager who leads by example, and tries to duplicate his or her own success in others; and those who burn out, give up managing, and return to strictly producing.

Because player managers receive little in the way of leadership training, many struggle to give away their authority. Some cling to their old expertise as a safety net. *I may not be the greatest leader, but I'm still the best salesperson, and they won't fire me if I'm producing sales.* Many player managers have a subconscious concern about carrying their weight, and they see empowering others as shirking part of their own duties. For others, being both manager and producer causes them to micromanage, resulting in a loss of employee trust, initiative, and creativity.

If your role involves both leading and applying your trade, remember your responsibility to prepare your organization's next leadership generation. Giving away your authority is far from a dereliction of duty. In fact, it *is* your duty.

# Chapter 5

Values-Based Leaders:
## Recognize the Best in Others

*"Seek out the bold, the strange, the misfits, the dreamers—and welcome their presence in our midst."*
-Tom Peters

After conducting performance and merit increase reviews on the anniversary date of an employee's hiring or promotion for years, one of my former employers switched to a focal point evaluation system instead. In doing so—by selecting a single annual date for all reviews—the company gained the ability to tie individual performance goals to the organization's objectives, and assess everyone within the same business cycle. To build excitement among the staff, senior management chose our existing company-wide celebration day as the yearly review date.

After the implementation, I observed an unexpected performance reaction in my staff. Immediately following the review process, productivity actually declined for several weeks. I initially attributed the trend to lingering suspicion among employees that they somehow lost money in the conversion.

Because employees received their reviews earlier or later than in prior years, maintaining equity required prorating raise percentages. And many employees struggled to understand the effect of that one-time occurrence. But when the performance pattern reappeared the second year, I searched for another reason.

I discovered that many employees redirected their focus in the weeks after the reviews. But why? The reviews included positive feedback and almost everyone earned raises, so why change direction now? Because, along with praise and appreciation, reviews typically included another element: suggestions for improvement. And after their reviews, employees concentrated all their attention on those suggestions, while basically discounting and ignoring the praise and appreciation they also received.

---

# Most organizations spend their training budgets on employee weaknesses—and miss the key to increasing productivity.

---

When striving for improvement, most of us do the same thing: we take our strengths for granted, and concentrate all our efforts on conquering our weaknesses. Those weaknesses may include shortcomings we perceive in ourselves, or flaws pointed out by our family, teachers, friends, or bosses.

We are not alone. The vast majority of organizations appear to believe that the best way for individuals to grow is to eliminate their weaknesses. So they instruct workers to recognize and focus on their deficiencies. They squander development budgets trying to fill perceived gaps in employees' skills. They structure performance evaluations to show limitations employees must overcome before they can get ahead. Is it any surprise that employee performance might decline, rather than improve, after we give them feedback that they—like us, we must admit—only pay attention to in its negative aspects?

The main fault rests with those in power, the leaders who are guiding their organizations. Why do so many leaders and their organizations fail to grasp their mistake and continue to miss the point of annual performance reviews—to *encourage the best* in their employees? One reason is that too many companies use outdated management tools, designed during the industrial revolution, which simply keep workers orderly and compliant. In a larger context, these companies have failed to adapt their leadership methods to the general movement away from physically dominated occupations in favor of knowledge-driven professions, instead.

In the predominantly manual labor environments of the past, effective techniques for measuring worker performance were largely nonexistent. Managers applied broadly based measurements, such as production line uptime or how many items a shift produced. The absence of function-driven measurements forced managers to grade individuals on subjective attributes—work quality or following directions—and attach predetermined labels like "meets expectations" or "needs immediate improvement." Despite advances in the performance-measuring sciences, evaluation practices that center around a supervisor's opinions and judgments prevail, even today.

Some managers are ill-equipped—as well as reluctant—to make the assessments these outdated appraisals require. They actually dread preparing and conducting performance reviews, so their employee evaluations are frequently overdue, if not overlooked altogether. All too often, these anxious reviewers make perfunctory efforts to complete the appraisal process—with demoralizing results. For instance, few supervisors record employee accomplishments throughout the year, and we know there is a human tendency is to recall negative events more readily than positive accomplishments. So when managers rely on memory, evaluations focus mainly on mistakes, failures, and weaknesses. Leaders need to change the way they look at measuring performance.

But new business models are emerging. The critical distinction between competing organizations is shifting away from the biggest over to the brightest; brains are replacing brawn, and we are outsourcing laborers while hiring knowledge workers. Leadership today requires skills for attracting, retaining, inspiring, and appraising a thinking workforce.

Unlike their manual-laboring predecessors, who responded to flawed review systems with collective bargaining, the knowledge workers are less willing to relinquish their individuality. Having opportunities to learn is what motivates the knowledge workers. They understand the value of knowledge and realize that the more knowledge they obtain, the greater their personal bargaining power. That's why organizations providing the greatest development opportunities maintain a competitive advantage in hiring and retaining today's knowledge workers.

But when your employees' thirst for knowledge collides with outdated, negatively biased performance review systems, you may as well kiss your productivity goodbye. You'll have workers wasting their time concentrating on overcoming subjectively identified weaknesses, rather than building on their proven strengths. And because your organization's competitive edge depends increasingly on your workers' knowledge, how you measure their performance is really critical to your success.

## Strengths versus Weaknesses

When we focus attention on employee weaknesses, we risk totally overlooking their strengths. Research from The Gallup Organization, reported in the book *Now, Discover Your Strengths* by Marcus Buckingham and Donald Clifton, shows how prevalent this tendency is.[1] Gallop asked 1.7 million workers in 101 companies from sixty-three countries the question, "At work do you have the opportunity to do what you do best every day?" Only 20 percent strongly agreed that they did.

---

# What prevents our employees from doing what they do best? Usually, our emphasis on what they do worst.

---

By focusing our attention on what our workers do poorly, we inhibit their growth—and limit their abilities to contribute their best efforts.

Let's look at an example. Suppose John is an accountant for a large organization. In addition to his fundamental duties of keeping a general ledger, he is responsible for anticipating the tax consequences of various business decisions. That involves preparing reports showing detailed what-if scenarios, complete with graphs and charts and data imported from other systems. For John, tax law knowledge and the ability to manipulate spreadsheets are job requisites.

John absolutely wows management with his technical skills in accounting as well as number crunching. What's more, he can recite every GAAP rule currently in effect and knows more about tax code than either H or R Block. But after his boss taps him to present year-end financial results at the annual shareholders' meeting, John stumbles through a slideshow that is both confusing and dull.

Along comes John's performance review. His boss commends his strengths in bookkeeping, report writing, and tax accounting, but condemns his PowerPoint deficiencies under "areas needing improvement." John learns his advancement depends on the ability to make public presentations, and is encouraged to take some upcoming classes on producing professional slideshows. He leaves the review wondering how he will ever manage to get ahead.

As John's boss, would you prefer he spent his time besieged with PowerPoint text boxes and slide transitions, or uncovering the next tax loophole that results in bottom line profits? My suggestion: let the graphic artists from the advertising department go crazy creating a multimedia extravaganza, and free John to concentrate on such accounting mysteries as treating extraordinary items and handling prior period adjustments.

In other words, recognize what work makes John salivate and unleash him to do what he does best. If he's strong in his core job requirements—great! Help him get even stronger. If he's weak in secondary roles, try to manage around those limitations. Leave the "areas needing improvement" section for the real problems—those affecting his core role.

You can't—and shouldn't—escape dealing with bona fide performance issues. But you'll know the difference when you see it. Suppose John routinely makes mistakes in rudimentary bookkeeping duties—debiting accounts he should credit, or something equally fundamental. In that scenario, managing around his weakness is both impractical and foolhardy.

But what if John simply enjoys doing certain tasks over others? Perhaps he avoids studying PowerPoint because he achieves more stimulation from figuring out how to capitalize interest costs. It may seem unwarranted, and even unfair, to reassign work he purposely avoids learning. But take a look at these startling statistics: Gallup found that employees sticking to their bailiwicks are 38 percent more likely to work in highly productive business units. There are other benefits to matching workers with what they do best: Gallop showed that employees are 50 percent more likely to work in business units with lower turnover and 44 percent more likely to work in business units with high customer satisfaction scores, when they think their employers are exploiting their best skills.[2]

Strive to match employees with jobs in which they can succeed and excel. That's when you will recognize—and capitalize on—the best in others.

## Watching Productivity Tick By

There's one simple way to recognize if you are overlooking your employees' best skills. If some of your workers are chronic clock watchers, there is a possibility they are under-challenged at work. According to Geoff Godbey, professor of leisure studies at Pennsylvania State University, clock watching is often an indicator of being over-qualified for the job. An article in the June 30, 2004, *Wall Street Journal* quotes Godbey: "When you're doing something and your skill and the challenge are closely aligned, you lose your sense of time."[3]

Employees want to feel important and useful. And they want to contribute their best talents to a worthwhile endeavor's success. "A chief complaint of workers isn't pay," says Godbey. "It's that they can't use their skills."

Paying attention to body language—listening with your eyes—might alert you to employees whose skills are underused.

## Geeks

Here's another way organizations mismatch worker skills and roles. Without the chance to demonstrate their best skills, four out of five employees believe they are in the wrong role at work. Identifying each person's strongest talents permits everyone the opportunity to contribute what they do best. But the sad truth is, when it comes to valuing our employees, we almost always prefer the generalists to the masters of one specific area.

---

## "Geeks are different from other people. If this comes as a shocking statement to you, you're either oblivious to others or unusually charitable with your opinion about others."
Paul Glen[4]

---

I am a computer geek by training, and although it has been awhile since I did geek work for a living, I am still a geek at heart. That's why I love Paul Glen's statement. And if you are both aware of others and reasonably generous in your judgments about humankind, you probably do know just how different computer geeks can be.

First, computer geeks have their own jargon. Just when you understand the difference between a megahertz and a megapixel, geeks start talking about *link rot* and *packet jams*. They use abbreviations and acronyms like JAVA, HTML, BIOS, XJACK, and SPD. They hold geeky titles like Deployment Specialist, Database Administrator, and Chief Knowledge Officer. I suspect that computer geeks contribute more to business jargon proliferation than any other profession. But what do you expect from the people who coined the term Y2K?

Speaking to a geek, even if you overcome the language barrier, can leave you dazed. Geekish speech is generally painfully slow. Pronunciation is exact. Word selection is meticulous. Computer programmers write code that deals with precise logic—if this, then that—and, as a result, negative questions seem to confuse them. "Aren't you able to fix my computer?" may generate a quizzical stare, some deep thought, and a bemusing answer. "No, I am not unable to fix your computer." Listeners may mistake the geek's dry sense of humor as annoyingly patronizing.

Similarly, punctuation purists might wince in disgust at structure geeks consider good form. Geeks commonly use punctuation that follows programming conventions—such as placing a sentence-ending period outside a quotation mark—rather than what they learned in Comp 101. Geeks also like typing in all caps or all lowercase letters. Using one writing standard for both programming and correspondence is easier, faster, and—to geeks—more logical.

But that's not all. Geeks are noncompliant; they resist mainstream or official authority structures. They respect technical knowledge far more than where a person resides on the organizational chart. The more proficient a geek is in applying technical knowledge, the higher that geek's status is among other techies. If the boss happens to be the smartest geek, that's great. Otherwise, informal leadership hierarchies will soon emerge.

## Appreciate geeks for what they contribute.

But, as leaders, we would prefer that geeks behave like the rest of us. That's why we spend training dollars trying to hone their oral and written communications skills. We counsel them about following the chain of command, and teach them that end-users (*We're their customers, damn it!*) deserve more respect and less condescension. Once those imperfections disappear, we tell ourselves, we'll all feel a lot better.

But wait. Consider this: our company geeks' personalities, even if grating to some, are immaterial to their productivity. So resist that urge to ship them off to seminars on conflict resolution or writing effective business letters; after all, when your computer crashes, whom do you call? Marketing? Instead, focus on exploiting and expanding their biggest attribute: their technical knowledge. To get the most from your training funds, send geeks to workshops on the latest in *security zones* or *alternative open-source browsers;* in other words, help them further develop their strengths, not flounder miserably in their non-strengths.

The computer field is not the only profession with geeks. In fact, various forms of geeks inhabit every organization. Ever sit through a meeting when an accounting geek explained the latest accounting rule change? *FASB 4,768 states that we must segregate, for income statement purposes, those fundraising dollars for which the donor received something of value from those that are simply donations. Now, I'm sure you'll find this part interesting...* I doubt that you will! Geeks exist in every profession.

Actually, I wish everyone were a geek in his or her profession. But if you find being a geek too disagreeable, how about becoming a master?

## Mastering the Best in You

Let's consider a few definitions of skill:

*Competent:*    properly or sufficiently qualified; adequate for the purpose

*Proficient:*    having an advanced degree of competence

*Master:*    an artist or performer of great and exemplary skill; a worker qualified to teach apprentices and carry on the craft independently

When we force our employees to strive for proficiency in everything, we miss the opportunity for them to achieve greatness or mastery in something—in the one area where they may, indeed, achieve just that. As the English proverb proclaims, "A jack of all trades is master of none."

## The pursuit of proficiency stifles our quest for mastery.

In *The Leading from the Heart Workshop*, participants take a quiz containing a dozen questions resembling those found on elementary and secondary education proficiency exams. The exercise tests participants' knowledge in math, history, geography, science, and spelling. Working alone, each person tries to answer as many questions as time allows.

Few participants—although educated professionals all—are able to remember the order of the planets, name the capital of every state beginning with the letters M and N, and spell *sacrilegious*. So after fifteen minutes, they partner with another person. Working together, partners solve more questions, as each contributes or corroborates answers. When partnerships remain stumped on certain questions, they merge to form larger teams, and continue to merge with others until they assemble enough knowledge to complete the test.

The exercise illustrates the unlikelihood that we as individuals will always know all the answers. Whereas some people are good at math, others excel in geography. It's the same in business, which is why organizations group employees by functions and expertise, like accounting, marketing, or sales. Why, then, are we so keen on finding corporate equivalents of the Renaissance person, or well-rounded employees who are proficient at multiple skills?

Imagine for a moment that you need a doctor. A general practitioner—the beloved family physician—can diagnose various conditions and treat many illnesses. A cardiologist specializes in treating heart disorders. A pediatric cardiologist treats children. A neonatal pediatric cardiologist cares for high-risk newborns. Which specialist you call will depend upon your needs at the time.

Without question, all doctors require extensive medical aptitude; but the more they specialize, the more their knowledge is concentrated. So, although your cardiologist is a highly skilled physician, you would hardly ask her to treat your sore throat.

Family physicians treat more patients than neonatal heart surgeons. Presented with that observation, a by-the-numbers business manager might react by hiring only general practitioners.

So why are hospitals creating new pediatric cardiac care units? Simply put, specialty medicine is highly profitable. By the same token, when organizations recognize the benefits of mastery, they find a cure for many business ailments.

I experienced the benefits of mastery firsthand. I began my career in banking as a computer programmer. As a generalist, I applied my trade to a wide-range of banking projects. However, I soon began specializing in checking account systems. I learned how to post checks and deposits to customer accounts, how to accrue and pay interest, and how to make all those transactions appear on monthly statements. As my programming knowledge grew, so did my understanding about how checks clear the federal banking system. I learned the banking regulations that affect checking accounts. I worked with the bank's backroom clerical staff to understand how they used our systems, and to discover ways I could make those systems easier for them to use. In short, I became a checking-account-system "master."

When the bank needed a new manager of deposit operations, they picked me. My expertise in checking accounts continued to grow: I learned the ins and outs of processing millions of account transactions each day. I developed finesse in handling customer complaints about service fees. And I learned the intricacies of stuffing account statements and cancelled checks, together, into envelopes. My mastery of checking accounts now included both the system and operational aspects.

Then, when the bank needed a salesperson to sell checking accounts to businesses, I convinced them to select me, again. Who better, I argued, to promote the benefits of our checking accounts than the person who helped design and program the checking account computer systems, and who oversaw the back-room deposit operations. Thanks to my mastery of every facet of checking accounts, the marketplace soon recognized me as an expert, and I was able to give my employer a competitive sales advantage over other banks.

So what's preventing companies from embracing mastery? In business, we tend to attribute competence—or lack thereof—to an employee's learning capacity. We further presume that what separates proficiency from competence is individual attitude and aptitude. But we tend to consider mastery out of reach, a level of attainment reserved for those few who possess natural intelligence, good fortune, or a head start. For example, we might assume mastering the company's computer system is something only the smartest employees, or those who can afford state-of-the-art computers at home, or those who started working with computers as young children, can do.

In his book *Mastery*, George Leonard wrote that mastery "is not really a goal or a destination but rather a process, a journey." Furthermore, Leonard proclaimed, "It's available to anyone who is willing to get on the path and stay on it—regardless of age, sex, or previous experience."[5]

If you are John the tax accountant, forget becoming proficient—or even competent—in slideshow preparation. Instead, concentrate on becoming John the tax *expert* who, in addition to understanding federal, state, and local taxes, knows the rules for every multinational taxing authority in existence. Then, focus your efforts on metamorphasizing into John the data-managing, cash-flow-forecasting, comparative-valuation-analyzing, mergers and acquisitions-evaluating, compensation-strategizing, and the-effects-of-all-of-the-above-on-taxes *guru*.

If you are a computer geek, let someone else attend the "Turning IT into Customer Service" workshop. You and your organization will benefit more if you master *multithreading* and *shared memory multiprocessors* than if you learn to kiss up to the users in the order entry department.

There is one exception to this "follow your skills" path; if you are both a player and a manager—a player manager—you must also master the craft of leadership. As we juggle our roles as leaders and producers, our tendency is to focus attention on our trade skills. *They won't fire me if I'm producing sales.* But once in a leadership role, you owe it to your employees, your organization, and yourself, to take whatever steps are necessary to lead effectively.

## Learning and Teaching Mastery

So what's the best method for helping employees become masters? Conventional education follows the intelligence theory model. Teachers give all students the same amount of time to learn a concept, and then attribute individual differences in learning to varying intelligence levels among students.

But in the early 1960s, cognitive abilities pioneer John B. Carroll introduced mastery learning. Carroll argued that each student requires more or less time than other students to learn the same material; therefore, success or failure depends on the amount of time allocated to learning, and not on each individual's learning capacity. We must allow each student, Carroll challenged, to learn at a highly individualized pace.[6]

However, most business organizations have not read Carroll's work. They still use the intelligence theory approach to learning. Employers set expectations—formal or informal—for the time required to learn a job. And they figure that those unable to achieve proficiency in the prescribed timeframe simply lack the necessary capacity. Two significant dangers are present in that mindset.

First, using a clock to measure individual progress places all responsibility for learning on the employee. We blame an employee's lack of growth on his or her inability to learn, when it is usually management's failure to provide sufficient training, guidance, or direction that's really at fault. Consequently, organizations tend to overrate managers while underrating employees.

Second, managers who are ignorant of Carroll's findings and who limit the time they will allow people to learn a role, are probably overlooking their employees' vastly underutilized potential to develop and grow. Disappointed in the results, they may set low expectations for their employees and feel the need to micromanage.

Of course, competence is the minimum requirement for every work role. Few organizations can afford the luxury of allowing workers unlimited time to learn the basic qualifications of their jobs. And once workers achieve competence, leaders must immediately instill the work ethic required to reach proficiency. But rather than pushing workers toward proficiency in several roles, values-based leaders encourage employees to master only the role they perform best.

Leonard has described the road to mastery in an unusual manner: it is, he says, a series of plateaus. You start with a burst of initial improvement. Then progress slows or declines slightly, and you settle at a plateau that is typically higher than where you started. After honing your skill, you experience another upward surge, before reaching the next plateau. More practice, more spurts. And more plateaus.

Wrote Leonard, "To take the master's journey, you have to practice diligently...you also have to be willing to spend most of your time on a plateau, to keep practicing even when you seem to be getting nowhere."[7]

Some view the plateaus as setbacks rather than milestones. Once their progress stalls, they accept a plateau as the limit of their learning capacity. In fact, you must cherish the plateaus, says Leonard. "To love the plateau is to love the eternal now, to enjoy the inevitable spurts of progress and the fruits of accomplishment, then serenely to accept the new plateau that waits just beyond them."[8]

## The ABCs of Differentiation

Alas, instead of paving a road to mastery, many organizations follow a dangerous path strewn with the latest corporate management trends. For example: Imagine a staff compiled entirely of the best employees in their fields. Consider your competitive advantage if every team member possessed great skills, a creative spirit, and a winning attitude. The obsession to assemble such an idyllic workforce led one in five *Fortune* 500 companies to implement an employee ranking system that is arguably the corporate equivalent of ethnic cleansing.[9]

The process has many names: differentiation, forced ranking, topgrading, and rank-and-yank. One prominent advocate, the leadership icon and former General Electric CEO Jack Welch, referred to it as a "vitality curve."[10] Whatever the euphemism, the practice is a systematic ranking technique that mandates turnover and creates turmoil.

## The objective of ranking employees seems noble: build the strongest, leanest workforce possible, while rewarding top performers.

Here's part of the rationale behind forced ranking: As businesses look for greater efficiencies, they tolerate underperformers less and less. When staff reductions are necessary, organizations need meaningful criteria for determining layoffs. From an employee perspective, ranking sends a strong message to top contributors expecting management to distinguish between those who contribute and those who merely get in the way. Is it any wonder that organizations are resorting to differentiation, forcing managers to rank employees against one another?

Although the protocol varies depending on the organization, differentiation works like this:

Write down all your staff members' names. Then objectively rank the individuals—from best to worst—in order of their performance and contribution to the organization. This is tricky, because job duties vary and employees have various levels of experience. But who are your top producers, your superstars? And who's underperforming?

Once you've completed the ranking process, circle the names representing the top 20 percent of your workers; these are your A players. Reward each with a big raise, a corner office, a coveted parking space, and a hug. If a hug is against the rules, give them more money. Hey, these are your best and brightest employees.

Next, look at the names in the middle 70 percent on your list. Those are your B players, the loyal grunts shouldering the majority of the heavy lifting. Grant them the obligatory annual cost-of-living increase, offer them heart-felt encouragement, and—if this year's budget allows—splurge on a little training to help them advance toward A-player status. But if a B player occupies an office with views in more than one compass direction, or walks less than fifty yards from the parking lot to the main entrance, you will want to take away those perks and give them to an A player.

Finally, circle the remaining names, the bottom 10 percent, to learn who your C players are. Fire them. Without exception. Time ran out for those workers—and for you to put off addressing their shortcomings any longer. Save your training dollars, rehabilitation efforts, and sympathy for someone more deserving, like a B player.

To complete the process, go out and hire new A players to replace the discarded C players. Then repeat regularly. Each cycle will naturally move you closer to a perfect workforce.

Sound cold? In his book, *Jack: Straight from the Gut,* Welch summarily dismissed criticism that the system is harsh. "Some think it's cruel or brutal to remove the bottom 10% of our people. It's just the opposite. What is brutal is keeping people around who aren't going to grow and prosper. There's no cruelty like waiting and telling people late in their careers that they don't belong—just when their job options are limited and they're putting their children through college or paying off big mortgages."[11]

But the system *is* cruel—to the employees told they don't belong, and to the managers responsible for executing it. The cruelty of differentiation results in declining morale, class action lawsuits, internal sabotage, and lost productivity.

Furthermore, differentiation absolutely fails to deliver the performance improvements its proponents promise. As JPMorgan Partners' Dana Beth Ardi said, "Glorifying the top 20 percent doesn't ensure you get the job done." Interviewed for Meredith Ashby's book *Leaders Talk Leadership*, Ardi adds, "It's not about the top; it's about finding the right combination of people to accomplish the mission."[12]

## The Dangers of Ranking

The primary difficulty in differentiation is finding—and maintaining—a standardized ranking methodology. Choosing appropriate criteria to use when ranking employees against one another is fraught with difficulties.

Says Ardi, "Some people are good at sales and marketing, some are great executors, some are loyal soldiers, some are really good customer relations types." Therefore, unless you judge employees in broad behavioral competencies—things like teamwork, initiative, and attitude—how can you rank employees serving in different roles?

> # Differentiation is more than unfair; it's downright ugly.

Determining rankings on highly subjective qualities naturally sparks controversies about fairness and consistency. In January 2000, Ford Motor Company implemented an employee ranking system that labeled 5 percent of the company's employees as C players. At the same time, Ford told employees garnering C rankings in two consecutive years that they faced either demotion or termination. Two class action lawsuits charged Ford with using the ranking system to force older, white employees out of the company in order to make way for younger and more culturally diverse workers. Ford paid $10.5 million to settle the suits.

In another instance, minority and female employees sued Microsoft Corporation, alleging the company's predominantly white male managers based forced ranking decisions on their own biases rather than merit. And Conoco employees asserted the company's ranking methods discriminated against American citizens and older workers when it laid off geophysicists and other scientists in 1999. [13]

Without specific, measurable, and well-communicated ranking criteria, employees will assume the worst about how differentiation decisions are determined. And when employees have those assumptions validated, as in the Ford case, they will lose trust in their leaders.

Another difficulty with forced ranking is that companies must identify the employees they are ranking, and decide against whom they're ranking them. Some organizations rank employees against coworkers in their own departments or divisions; others against peers throughout the organization. It might seem an insignificant consideration. But differentiation assumes that employees in a group form a normal bell curve, with a few exceptional and inferior performers surrounding a large number of average performers. Such patterns may exist in companies with hundreds or thousands of employees, but problems arise when trying to apply this statistical approach to small groups.

This is a critical point: the ramifications of division versus company-wide ranking are potentially enormous. The wrong method can mask poor performance or cheat high achievers out of earned rewards. And otherwise average or sub-par workers can rise to the top in groups of underperforming workers. Conversely, individuals considered outstanding or satisfactory in a company-wide ranking might rate as underperformers if they work among other very good people.

Those leaders who are leading from the heart find differentiation particularly unpleasant. Some managers are reluctant to classify any employees as low performers, especially after the initial rounds. Identifying and firing underperformers is easiest in the first round when managers address the lingering problems they know they've avoided. But then what? Once companies dismiss their obvious problem employees, identifying a fixed number of workers to fire every year is onerous. However, managers finding differentiation too distasteful soon discover themselves in the C-player category.

Meanwhile, managers attempting to protect their employees might do so by inflating performance reviews, engaging in horse trading with other managers, or resorting to outright deception. Some managers wait to fire problematic employees until ranking time, thereby ensuring their own C-player pipeline. At General Electric, some managers circumvented the system by classifying retiring employees, terminated workers, and—in one instance—a man dead for two months, as C players.

According to Welch, "Making the judgments is not easy, and they are not always precise. Yes, you'll miss a few stars and a few late bloomers—but your chances of building an all-star team are improved dramatically." On the other hand, Ardi says, "Some of the underperformers may be the jewels in the rock that you have to mine and develop."

Of course, retaining poor performers is unacceptable; leaders must show underachievers that hard work is required, and they must reward top performers for extraordinary efforts. Asking workers to meet or exceed high standards fosters growth in both the employees and the organization. But when employees face a forced ranking system that increases competition among coworkers, teamwork and collaboration give way to hostility. Workers are less apt to help one another or share information, and more inclined to sabotage one another's work. And when the ranking process appears biased or skewed, employees feel powerless to meet the expectations necessary to avoid termination.

## The Forgotten Worker Bs

Perhaps the most dangerous consequence of differentiation is that we take for granted our so-called B players, those unsung champions whose knowledge, commitment, and stability form the foundation of our organizations. While management glorifies superstars, and fires and replaces the weak, it ignores the majority in the middle.

These core employees steadily carry out our corporate missions. They show up every day, often serving on the front lines. They change jobs infrequently—it's improbable that anyone will consider B players for promotions—so they know the ins and outs of the organization and understand its culture. They steer clear of company politics. Since they care more about their work than their careers, they are willing to challenge the status quo. (Semmelweis was certainly not an A player—he was an assistant physician in an unglamorous setting, yet he took on the entire medical establishment.) And because they get little attention, they are highly self-sufficient.

---

# Differentiation focuses our attention away from the mainstream workforce, and puts valuable people at risk.

---

Many "average" workers are highly skilled, dedicated professionals for whom money, authority, and power are uninspiring.

Often, all that separates them from A-player status is a reluctance to sacrifice their personal lives for ambition; they'll deliver an A-level performance as long as they can avoid a workaholic schedule. Some make a midlife renouncement of the fast track; they still find hard work satisfying, but prefer scaling new personal heights to clambering up the corporate ladder.

Despite a characteristic aversion to drawing attention to their individual needs, average workers crave recognition just like self-obsessed top performers. And when average workers are struggling—just like underachievers—they need nurturing. Without attention, they may wonder if you've labeled them C players, proceed to fall out of alignment with the organization's mission, and eventually leave.

Dana Beth Ardi says, "Some of those people who fall in the middle ranges of top-grading can turn out to be your breakaway 'A' players once you put them in the right seats." So leave differentiation to organizations like General Electric: someday, even they will see the light.

## Forcing Forced Ranking

The most overlooked aspect of the whole idea of ranking is the frustration that leads many companies to implement differentiation in the first place. The term *forced ranking* says it all. It highlights deeper leadership issues—specifically, issues with managers who fear singling people out for outstanding efforts, who fail to address poor performance, and who neglect their duty to fire employees when necessary. If, as the name implies, we must force managers to perform these aspects of their jobs, they are ill-equipped for their leadership roles to begin with. On the other hand, substituting a mandate for training destroys leadership effectiveness, and makes the organization itself the ultimate micromanager.

## Alternate Career Paths

In his book *The Peter Principle*, sociologist Laurence Johnston Peter introduced his now-familiar hierarchical incompetence theory.[14] Dr. Peter observed that people within an organization tend to advance beyond their competence levels. Here's how it works: once workers prove competent in their jobs, we inevitably promote them. When they display competence at the next level, we promote them again. We repeat the process until each employee reaches a position for which he or she is consummately unqualified.

Furthermore, as *The Peter Principle* reveals, after we promote people to their levels of incompetence, they remain in place. Since organizations seldom fire or demote top officials, explained Peter, incompetent people typically occupy the highest ranks of organizations.

A primary cause of "The Peter Principal" in action is the up-or-out promotion philosophy of many organizations. Because the prevailing organizational mentality is that everyone aspires to be the boss, workers are required to assume leadership responsibilities in order to advance in salary or rank. Traditional career paths compel employees to trade their technical competencies for the status and financial rewards that companies reserve for middle managers.

Although most people want recognition for their efforts, influence over how their work is accomplished, and opportunities to display their creativity and have autonomy, the truth is many workers lack the desire to lead others. Frederick W. Smith, CEO of FedEx, warns, "Many organizations get in trouble in this regard, because the only avenue they have for financially rewarding top performers is to move them into management positions."[15]

Smith suggests, "You have to have rewarding, alternate career paths for outstanding specialists—engineers, for example, or R&D people—who can continue to make major contributions to the organization without going into management." And talent-driven companies are doing just that. New titles like Specialist, Master, and Fellow describe experts with deep knowledge and experience in their crafts. Their qualifications include demonstrated experience and expertise, as well as credentials from the applicable professional organizations. Values-based organizations are creating opportunities for experienced practitioners, those for whom leadership holds little appeal, to grow within the jobs they love and do best.

This trend introduces enormous benefits. Companies recognize savings in training and increased workforce stability. Specialists get seats at the decision-making table, alongside those following a management track. Because specialists are uninterested in acquiring power, competition with their ambitious colleagues is nonexistent and teamwork improves. Viable career path alternatives also make the organization more attractive to qualified job seekers.

Best of all, this approach foils "The Peter Principle" of promoting employees into positions for which they simply don't have the skills, and instead empowers employees to strive for mastery in the area where their true skills lie.

## Internal Candidates

Another area where organizations are typically making a major mistake is in following a disturbing trend in hiring. Rather than recognizing the best within our organizations, it is fashionable to believe that the choicest employees are somewhere else—"out there." Perhaps employees from our competitors hold added intrigue, as if, once hired, they will eagerly divulge the trade secrets of their former employers. Maybe we think they will introduce new approaches—better than anything we might be doing—or inject refreshing, unwavering attitudes. Or possibly, if they are already performing our kind of work, we hope to save time and money on training.

## Organizations behave as if the best employees are working somewhere else.

I always questioned this thinking. For instance, if the salespeople at competing banks surpassed ours, why did we consistently outperform them? Actually, because our competition mustered little opposition, I would sooner leave their employees in place. I favored filling my openings with candidates from inside the organization—people like Dave Koenig.

Before I tell you about Dave, though, let me describe what qualifications I looked for when hiring a salesperson. I always found that outstanding salespeople spend more time listening to prospective customers than talking to them. As a result, they can sense what people are thinking by interpreting oral and nonverbal reactions. Understanding how their organization's systems work is also essential; I have watched too many salespeople oversell—or undersell—their company's capabilities. And, especially in competitive industries, there are times when salespeople need the backbone to stand by their price.

Dave possessed all those attributes when I recruited him from another department. His only deficiency was actual sales experience. You see, Dave headed the bank protection department. His duties included investigating and preventing customer fraud, apprehending employees who stole money, maintaining surveillance systems, teaching tellers how to survive robberies, and filling out suspicious activity reports. How, skeptics wanted to know, did that background prepare him for an occupation peddling banking services to government agencies, school systems, universities, and nonprofit organizations?

As a former police officer, Dave was a skillful interrogator. More than once, I watched him artfully elicit signed confessions from dishonest employees, asking a few disarming questions at first, and then listening while they revealed their sins. And, by reading their body language, he could detect when suspected scoundrels were withholding information or lying outright. I knew those skills would prove invaluable in sales; discerning when a customer is being disingenuous can save wasted effort, and recognizing misstated objections can help pinpoint actual concerns.

As an investigator, Dave knew his way around the bank's computer systems. He had command of the technology, knew where records were kept, and understood how account transactions flowed. I was certain Dave could clarify our procedures to prospects, and respond to endless customer requests for information.

When dealing with deceitful people, Dave was direct. When he caught them, he told them. When they argued, or pleaded for one more chance, he stood his ground. Therefore, I knew when it came to pricing, he would have profitable discussions.

Today, Dave is a vice president of public funds for a *Fortune* 500 bank, and he is one helluva salesperson.

I must add that I owe much of my leadership success to shamelessly poaching employees from other departments. I stayed alert for hard workers who appeared restless in their current jobs. Having observed the various work ethics of many coworkers for years, I knew who contributed the most. If they carried baggage—perhaps some viewed them as "disrespectful" because they frequently challenged the status quo, a trait I saw as appealing—odds were I already knew what was inside that baggage. And I sought out the best.

I firmly believe it is easier to teach someone how to do a job than how to fit a culture. So I often pursued nontraditional candidates like Dave, individuals lacking job-specific skills, but who demonstrated values already in alignment to the corporation. And if they also showed strengths like creativity, initiative, and perseverance, I would gladly invest time teaching them specialized job functions. Besides, like most veterans, the ones I swiped had long-established personal networks that enabled them to get things done.

I found hiring from within faster and cheaper; rarely did I place ads in the Sunday newspaper and wait for a trickle of résumés, or pay an exorbitant recruiter fee. More importantly, hiring from within boosts morale; it telegraphs proof that opportunities exist for advancement, and it creates movement for people seeking those advanced openings.

Even differentiation proponents recommend internal hiring. Bradford Smart, author of *Topgrading*, wrote, "Historically, premier companies have 'grown their own.' They promote people they have worked with, and these people know the company well and understand jobs to which they are promoted. So, 'promote from within' results in a much higher success rate than can external recruiting."[16]

Stop looking out there for your next successful hire. Your best candidates are likely right here, already coming to work for you each and every day!

# Chapter 6

## Have a Vision and
## Convince Others to Share It

*"George wears his passions on his sleeve. He needs to learn to hide his emotions from his employees."*
**-From every performance review I've ever gotten**

In 1992, Sears, Roebuck and Company suffered its worst financial year in history. The company lost $3.9 billion, with 75 percent of the shortfall attributed to its retail group. Over the next three years, senior management devised a massive turnaround strategy to transform the retailer's marketing and return the company to sustainable profitability. But, in order for their initiative to succeed, management knew it needed to engage each and every one of Sears' 300,000 employees.[1]

Sears' management recognized that showing employees a connection between their personal efforts and the company's business objectives was critical to improving customer service. In fact, its measurements showed that when employees felt connected to the outcome, they remained with the company longer, provided better customer service, and even recommended Sears more frequently to families and friends.

To gauge how well employees understood the company's customer service objectives, one high-ranking Sears official visited stores all across the nation, asking hundreds of workers along the way to describe their primary responsibility. Over half said they believed their jobs were to protect company assets. *Protect company assets?* Who talks like that? Well, actually, management talks like that. Thus, Sears realized management had programmed the company's retail salespeople to behave more like security guards than customer service ambassadors.

Sears' experience is typical. In its 2002 study, Watson Wyatt found that less than half—just 49 percent—of all workers understand their organization's business objectives.[2] How can you increase revenues if over half your sales force thinks its most important duty is policing shoplifters?

Too many business leaders lack the essential ability to articulate the big picture to their workforce: their messages are devoid of emotion, energy, excitement, and any mention of values. Is it any surprise that only 32 percent of respondents in the Watson Wyatt study said senior management motivates them to perform well?

Under the widespread illusion that reciting financial data somehow inspires performance, managers behave like walking-talking annual reports. *Net profit this quarter is up 20 percent over the same period last year. But we're still below budget and need everyone's added effort.* In fact, too much spoken emphasis on financial results can backfire on leaders. When the same Sears official asked salespeople how much profit each thought the company netted on a dollar of revenue, the median guess was forty-five cents—a far cry from the 2 percent profit the company actually earned. And Sears found that those employees who overestimated the retailer's profit margin were less trustful of management and more resistant to change. So messages portraying management as having an unquenchable thirst for higher sales and wider profits leaves workers feeling cynical and distrustful.

Without an inspiring vision from their leaders, employees will struggle to discern any link between their private ambitions and the company's actual mission. And leaders who fail to communicate messages that inspire trust will find leadership unnecessarily difficult.

---

# The days of dictating work and mandating change are long gone.

---

To lead effectively, you must inspire the behavior you are seeking. Values-based leaders identify shared aspirations—that is, they show how aligning with the purpose of the enterprise will help employees achieve their own goals and meet their own needs. Once workers see that connection, they can stop wondering and start contributing to the organization's ultimate success.

The best leaders imagine a future that is in someway better than the present. We call those mental images visions. Especially appealing to your employees are visions embracing values found in the organization's mission statement. Your ability to ennoble even clichéd business goals will inspire your employees to help you meet company objectives.

If your business wants to increase sales, you could show employees the connection between the company's revenues and its stock price. Or you could try what Sears did early in its turnaround, when a special task force surveyed 80,000 Sears employees to identify what they valued most. The top six responses were honesty, integrity, individual respect, teamwork, trust, and customer focus. Funny, they forgot to mention higher sales! Knowing employees valued customer service—long a trademark value at Sears—and armed with the knowledge that half misunderstood their roles, company leaders presented workers with a customer-focused vision: "Make Sears a compelling place to shop." That vision assured employees of a shared interest in service excellence, and reiterated that helping customers make purchases is their primary role. In 1993, just one year after its near-demise, Sears had one of its best financial performances ever, increasing merchandise sales by 9 percent, while producing a total shareholder return of 56 percent.

Is your objective to reduce production costs? You might explain to employees how defective work increases expenses, and even threaten them with reprimand when errors occur. Instead, what if you shared your vision of being the team with the highest quality rankings in your division, the whole company, or even the entire marketplace?

Perhaps your industry is highly regulated. You could post the rules—and the penalties for breaking them—for all to see. But finding themselves drawn to your company because of its stated commitment to promoting morals, ethics, and trust, employees would find more inspiration in your vision for a principle-centered organization, one that complies simply because it's the right thing to do.

Down deep, employees know they are responsible for increasing sales, lowering costs, and obeying government regulations. But inspiring those actions is difficult—instructing people to sell more and maximize profits for invisible shareholders generates zero emotional appeal. On the other hand, asking employees who are attracted to the company's customer-centered focus to provide outstanding service is highly inspiring. And inspiration is the real secret to values-based leadership.

So where do you begin? You start by having a vision.

## Have a Vision

Visionary leaders hold pictures of what the future can be in their minds. Values-based leaders use those mental portraits to navigate their lives. Guided by their visions, values-based leaders are so intent on reaching their goals that others are simply compelled to follow.

Sometimes, a vision is a leader's own idea. Other times, a leader embraces an existing idea and focuses additional attention on it. Regardless of the source, visions always involve the future and, in this way, inspire forward progress. Yet visionary leaders see things backwards: they envision the result first, and *then* they develop a strategy to get there.

To show you the incredible power that having a vision can bring to bear in achieving any goal, the following stories describe three ordinary individuals, their extraordinary visions, and their spirited efforts to make them reality.

## Asa Philip Randolph

On August 28, 1963, 250,000 civil rights devotees assembled on the mall surrounding the Lincoln Memorial. They came to the nation's capital to participate in one of the largest nonviolent demonstrations in history. Most Americans remember the event for its closing address, delivered by a thirty-four-year-old southern Baptist minister named Martin Luther King, Jr. "I Have a Dream," King told the country, that day.

Labor leader and civil-rights activist Asa Philip Randolph had conceived the march twenty years earlier.[3] In 1925, Randolph formed the Brotherhood of Sleeping Car Porters, the first African American trade union, to bargain for improved working conditions for the porters of the Pullman Company. He began organizing the March on Washington Movement in 1941 to protest discriminatory hiring practices in the wartime defense industry.

Having devised the demonstration to pressure Franklin D. Roosevelt to intervene, Randolph called it off when the president at last issued an executive order barring discrimination in both armament industries and federal agencies.

In 1962, the country suffered an economic recession. Twice as many African Americans were unemployed than whites; over one and a half million African Americans were looking for work. Two decades after he initially envisioned his march on the capital, Randolph again contemplated an epic Washington rally. Now an older man in his seventies, he began talking to long-time friend and strategist Bayard Rustin about a massive but peaceful protest.

## Asa Philip Randolph first devised the March on Washington Movement in 1941.

Meanwhile, events in 1963, the year marking the Emancipation Proclamation's centennial anniversary, caused Martin Luther King, Jr., to contemplate his own grand demonstration. That spring, police in Birmingham, Alabama, arrested King for marching in a parade, held him in solitary confinement, and refused his right to legal counsel. In June, President John F. Kennedy sent Congress a civil rights bill. King knew a large televised demonstration in Washington could impel Congress to endorse the legislation, and he instructed his aides to approach Randolph about collaborating.

Randolph and Rustin originally planned to lobby for a new federal jobs program and a higher minimum wage. But the newsworthiness surrounding King's Birmingham incarceration, and the urgency of the pending Kennedy bill expanded their agenda. Appropriately, they named the protest the "March on Washington for Jobs and Freedom."

Critics and supporters alike tried to persuade Randolph to cancel the march. Although he publicly supported the demonstration, Kennedy privately warned, "We want success in Congress, not just a big show at the Capitol. Some of these people are looking for an excuse to be against us; and I don't want to give any of them a chance to say 'Yes, I'm for the bill, but I am damned if I will vote for it at the point of a gun.'" FBI director J. Edgar Hoover tried to dampen support for the rally by defaming King and Rustin. And on the morning of the march, Hoover ordered his agents to telephone known celebrity participants and advise them to withdraw. But Randolph had waited long enough.

Demonstrators came to Washington by car, bus, train, and airplane. Although the marchers were predominantly African American, people of all races, religions, and social standings participated. Whereas some public figures and luminaries attended, most participants were everyday people—standing in what King later called "majestic dignity." All three major networks televised the march, one of the first events broadcast live via satellite around the world.

Randolph opened the program by saying, "Fellow Americans, we are gathered here in the largest demonstration in the history of this nation. Let the nation and the world know the meaning of our numbers. We are not a pressure group, we are not an organization or a group of organizations, we are not a mob. We are the advance guard of a massive moral revolution for jobs and freedom."

Critics forecasted riots, but those fears proved unwarranted. Political commentator Russell Baker noted the civility of the enormous, diverse congregation, writing in the *New York Times*, "No one could remember an invading army quite as gentle as the two hundred thousand civil-rights marchers who occupied Washington today. The sweetness and patience of the crowd may have set some sort of national high-water mark in mass decency."

After the marchers left the Mall, Rustin found Randolph standing alone on the stage. "Mr. Randolph," said Rustin, "it looks like your dream has come true."

Through his tears, Asa Philip Randolph proclaimed it "the most beautiful and glorious day" of his life.

## Billy Starr

By age twenty-five, Billy Starr had already lost his mother, an uncle, and a cousin to cancer. An avid rock climber, hiker, and cyclist, he had often turned to sports for solace.[4]

Soon after his forty-nine-year-old mother died, Starr joined three friends on a hike along the Appalachian Trail. Freezing rain pummeled the hikers for the entire first week, forcing his companions to retreat. But after conquering the 400-mile trail alone, Starr reflected on more than just his physical accomplishment. He had learned about mental toughness and the importance of having a purpose for his efforts. And when, after a particularly grueling stretch, a stranger offered him coffee, Starr realized how even small generous acts could lift the spirits of someone in need.

Starr began a personal ritual in 1977.[5] Once each year, he would rise before dawn and embark on a punishing bike ride from Boston to Provincetown. His goal: complete the 140-mile journey in time to catch the afternoon ferry back home. The annual tradition led to an idea. He would ask friends to participate in a long-distance cycling adventure to raise money for cancer research.

On a Saturday morning in 1980, Starr led three dozen friends on a bike trip across the state of Massachusetts. Two days—and 220 miles—later, after getting lost and running out of food, the thirty-six exhausted bikers had raised over $10,000 for cancer research.

---

# "I'm going to make this big."

### Billy Starr

---

Starr donated the proceeds to the Jimmy Fund to support the battle against cancer at Boston's Dana-Farber Cancer Institute. The fund's namesake was a twelve-year-old cancer patient named Einar Gustafson. A patient of chemotherapy pioneer Dr. Sidney Farber, Gustafson appeared on a 1948 national broadcast of Ralph Edwards's *Truth or Consequences* radio show. Transmitted from his hotel room, the appeal raised over $200,000. Producers gave Gustafson the moniker "Jimmy" to protect his identity, thus the name Jimmy Fund.[6]

On Sunday night, with all the bikers safe and sound, Starr turned to a friend and said, "I'm going to make this big." With that prophetic statement, the Pan-Massachusetts Challenge began.

The annual three-day event now draws nearly 4,000 cyclists from across the United States, Europe, and Asia. In its first twenty-five years, the Pan-Massachusetts Challenge donated $120 million to the Jimmy Fund, contributing nearly half the fund's yearly revenue. Sharing his Appalachian Trail lesson about the need for purpose, Starr encourages participants to commit as much energy to fundraising as they do to preparing for the ride's physical hardships. As a result, the challenge raises more than twice the money of any other athletic fundraising event in the country.

Writing in the Op-Ed section of the *Boston Globe*, Starr touched on the importance of having a purpose. "A unified force of people made whole by the belief in a single mission has the ability to improve the human condition."[7] Early on, he realized that something far greater than a fundraising event had emerged. Participants found inspiration in the opportunity to help others. They shared their passion with families, friends, and coworkers, and in turn, others wanted to contribute. Now, thousands of volunteers donate their time and talents to the event.

Says Starr, "At the Pan-Massachusetts Challenge, we like to say that when you ask people to donate money or time to a cause, you are empowering them to feel good about themselves. This is, perhaps, among the greatest gifts anyone can give another human being."

## Ann Bancroft

Ann Bancroft led her first Antarctic expeditions at the age of eight, albeit make-believe ones. In a snowy field behind her home in southern Minnesota, she played out the stories she had read—about the adventures of explorer Ernest Shackleton. Before long, she guided her cousins on wintry pilgrimages into the imaginary frozen plains of her family's backyard. Thirty years later, Bancroft's own real-life explorations inspired millions of children.[8]

Bancroft earned a degree in physical education from the University of Oregon while struggling with dyslexia. Although she continued to enjoy the outdoors—especially the cold and snow—on weekends and vacations, she settled into her stable vocation of teaching elementary school in Minneapolis. In 1986, world-renowned polar explorer Will Steger recruited Bancroft for a thousand-mile dogsled expedition. While on that trip, she became the first known woman in history to reach the North Pole.

Inspired by this remarkable achievement, Bancroft left teaching to concentrate on her dream of leading an all-women expedition. In 1993, she led a four-woman team on an attempt to cross

Antarctica on skis. Unable to line up cash sponsors in advance, Bancroft forged ahead anyway, hoping corporate supporters would emerge in the wake of a successful expedition. But the sixty-seven-day journey ended when a team member's illness forced them to abandon the mission at the South Pole. Despite holding the distinction as the first woman to reach both poles, it took Bancroft seven years to repay the debt from the aborted voyage.

While exploring Antarctica, Bancroft first learned about a Norwegian explorer named Liv Arnesen. Planning her own trek to the South Pole, Arnesen wrote Bancroft seeking her advice. In February 2001, the two women teamed up to sail and ski across Antarctica's land mass, completing the 1,717-mile trek in ninety-four days.[9]

---

## "I'm always wondering, how will I act at my moment of truth?"
### Ann Bancroft

---

Reaching this extraordinary milestone for women was not without its hardships. At one point, Arnesen fell through a thin layer of ice obscuring what seemed a bottomless hole; catching herself on the edge, she narrowly averted disaster. Bancroft endured agonizing pain caused by a torn shoulder muscle. Each woman lost nearly twenty pounds.

Although it was just the two of them facing dangerous natural elements, they were far from alone. More than three million schoolchildren around the world followed their expedition on the Internet. Bancroft and Arnesen spoke by satellite telephone with classrooms in Minnesota. Students asked questions about Antarctica, about its geography and climate, and about how the women coped.

Though they had hoped to travel another 400 miles and cross over the entire continent, the women ran out of time. The Antarctic summer drew to an end, and days of total darkness approached. Unavoidable whiteout blizzard conditions would endanger the lives of rescuers should something go wrong. Meanwhile, a tragedy would affect the millions of children rooting for their safe return. They made the difficult and emotional decision to end the excursion.

Steger, quoted in an article in the September 2004 issue of *Fast Company,* commended them for their courageous choice.[10] "Doing what Ann and Liv did is much harder than reaching the peak of the mountain, flying a flag, and saying, 'We're heroes, take us to the parade.' Real leadership is not about getting to the top. In this game, leadership is about coming back alive."

Bancroft continues to explore her dreams. "For me," she told *Fast Company*, "exploration is about that journey to the interior, into your own heart. I'm always wondering, how will I act at my moment of truth? Will I rise up and do what's right, even if every fiber of my being is telling me otherwise?"

As these three stories illustrate, visions have fantastic power, whether you are trying to influence a million people, motivate a single employee, or find the internal fortitude to finish what you started. All three visionaries found inspiration in their ideas. What's more, their personal visions impacted the lives of millions.

Randolph's dream for a peaceful labor protest inspired a quarter of a million people to leave their homes and journey to Washington, D.C. Inspired, in turn, by the audience's size and peaceful, dignified decorum, King set aside his prepared address and launched into the famous remarks that would move people forever. And the ongoing role King's enduring message plays in reversing hatred and ending discrimination toward African Americans is immeasurable.

Starr imagined gathering some friends for a weekend bike-a-thon to raise funds for cancer research. But rather than relaxing once he had accomplished his goal, he expanded his earlier vision. As a result, thousands of participants and volunteers raise millions of dollars every year, and provide hope to hundreds of thousands of cancer patients. More than that, Starr's efforts have inspired countless others worldwide to organize or partake in fundraising events to help people in need.

As a child, Bancroft envisioned herself as a great adventurer. She helped Steger fulfill his vision when she explored the North Pole with him in 1986. Her personal vision became leading an all-female team across Antarctica. Later, she shared a vision with Arnesen. Each time her vision was clear: go first. Bancroft's accomplishments occupy the daydreams of schoolchildren, and fuel the aspirations of future explorers everywhere.

## Your vision = your values.

Making your organization's vision your own is the key to living by the values you profess. If the mission statement claims your company strives to provide excellent service, you must have a vision to make that a reality. Your vision, wrapped around the mission statement's values, reinforces for workers your commitment to those values.

But you must have a starring role in your vision. Had Bancroft simply declared, "Someone ought to lead a team of women across the Antarctic," few would have paid attention. Instead, she declared it her own personal goal to lead that expedition. For people to follow your inspiring vision, you must lead the way.

You might consider yourself incapable of envisioning heroic acts on the scale of individuals like Randolph, Starr, or Bancroft. But, in point of fact, all three began with small goals. Randolph originally hoped to provoke politicians into action. Starr initially looked to add meaning to his lengthy bike rides. Bancroft was chasing her childhood fantasies. Ultimately, their ability to convince others to share their visions is what made them remarkable.

## And Convince Others to Share It

Critical to values-based leadership are the skills needed to communicate powerfully a vision's significance. The ability to share their vision separates mavericks from malcontents. Semmelweis may have had a vision—to eradicate the avoidable spreading of disease—but he lacked the skills to appeal successfully to his colleagues. By developing the talent to appeal and convince, leaders can build into their messages those enticing images that so inspire others to follow.

If you think that conveying ideas effectively is an innate ability—a talent reserved for naturally gifted orators—then you are probably neglecting your role as a communicator. In fact, vision sharing involves two separate—yet interdependent—and learnable skills. The first is the ability to identify, or frame, your organization's goals; depending on your situation, someone might have already done that. The second is the ability to express those goals using emotionally stimulating and memorable language. Whereas the framed message describes the vision, your language must clarify and expand upon its appeal to determine what impression you leave with your listeners. (King's framed message was an appeal for racial equality, but he chose language that described his "dream.") Furthermore, you can master the art of vision sharing by learning how to select appropriate language.

If leadership communication is all about language, maybe you should just hire a speech writer to prepare your remarks to employees. Preposterous yes, but I know CEOs who enlist their marketing staffs to prepare speeches for personnel pep rallies, management meetings, even holiday toasts. But unless you only communicate with employees from behind a podium, you need more than canned speeches to share your vision.

Make your vision a part of all your conversations with employees.

## Emphasize Common Values

An inspiring vision embodies values with strong appeal for its entire audience. The vision then calls attention to those common values and illustrates how—and why—all the individuals in that audience can connect.

When your employees came on board, they saw a bond between their personal values and those listed in the organization's mission statement. When reinforced, those common values give their jobs meaning and purpose.

> # A stimulating vision must embody values with strong appeal to everyone.

Let's say your manufacturing company's mission statement promises that "We strive to minimize the safety risks to our employees" as well as that "We focus on maximizing earnings for our investors." Of course, there are financial benefits to limiting accidents in the workplace, but your company actually cares about keeping employees safe. So how do you promote both values?

The spontaneous tendency of most managers is to concentrate on the financial viewpoint. So you might preach how "safety is good business," important to keeping expenses low and profits high. You could create a PowerPoint presentation illustrating how on-the-job accidents affect the bottom line, showing the financial effects of lost productivity, wages paid to injured workers and substitute employees, equipment repair costs, insurance claims, increased insurance premiums, and fines. But how can you expect employees to glean your genuine concern for them from that approach?

When Paul O'Neill became CEO of Alcoa in 1987, he saw an opportunity to prove what he already knew—that is, values and business objectives can coexist even in the largest corporations. He believed a company could ensure financial success by concentrating on its core values.[11]

Above all, O'Neill valued worker safety. As he pointed out, "When human beings are hurt physically, nothing else matters." On his first day at Alcoa, he met with his new safety director who boasted about the company's unusually low number of days lost from accidents. O'Neill said that was great, but promised the safety director that going forward the company would have zero lost work day cases.[12] Then he set out to make Alcoa a safer company.

O'Neill sensed that long-time Alcoa executives privately predicted the economic realities of the aluminum industry would inevitably force him to abandon his vision. So, on a tour of one of the company's oldest plants, he reiterated his vision of being the safest company in the world to everyone present—to management, union leaders, and hourly employees. He instructed managers to fix any identified safety hazards immediately, regardless of the monetary cost. He handed out his home telephone number and invited workers to call him if their managers failed to comply. He made it clear his vision was unshakeable.

In a 2002 speech at the University of Pittsburgh's Berg Center for Ethics and Leadership, O'Neill said his emphasis on safety united the employees. "The 140,000 of us were connected on something that was not about money, and it was not about doing something for the company. It was about demonstrating in a tangible way that we could achieve incredibly important goals that were meaningful to individuals."[13]

Remember, you want to emphasize those values common to your organization and your employees. Listing profit as a business objective in the mission statement is honorable; however, few job applicants come to your organization because its mission is to multiply shareholder value. Winning the hearts of safety-minded employees is difficult if you are going to measure the cost of their well-being in dollars and cents. Demonstrating that their safety takes priority over profits proves you share a common goal: returning every worker home safely, every night.

Stressing common values also has the added benefit of helping to resolve internal conflicts between divisions or departments. For instance, salespeople might say, "Those people in operations are unwilling to go the extra mile to please my customers." Meanwhile, the operations people complain, "The salespeople go out and promise special procedures without checking with us first." Emphasizing common values reminds people we're all in this together. Although his "I Have a Dream" speech addressed the plight of African Americans, King intentionally stressed values important to everyone: liberty, equality, and freedom. He made it easy for all Americans to relate, by drawing on familiar lines from the Constitution, the Declaration of Independence, and the song "America."

What are your organization's primary values? Which ones have the strongest mutual appeal for the organization and individual employees? What connections can you establish? Answering those questions is the first step in identifying language that will emphasize common values.

## Describe the Importance of the Values

Explaining why the organization's values are important helps people connect emotionally with your vision. Visions with the greatest impact depict the status quo as intolerable, and alternative values as unacceptable. And by stressing a problem's seriousness and the urgency for change, you portray your vision as the only suitable approach.

---

# Does management mean what it says, or is the mission statement just a marketing slogan?

---

The introduction of DNA technology helped overturn untold numbers of criminal convictions in Illinois. Alarmingly, by January 2003, Illinois had exonerated seventeen wrongfully convicted death row inmates. While Governor, George Ryan put a moratorium on executions and commissioned a panel to make suggestions for mending the state's death penalty system. However, the legislature failed to enact the committee's recommendations. That month, in his final days in office, Ryan commuted the death sentences of 167 men and women on death row.

Announcing his decision in a speech to the Northwestern University College of Law, Ryan explained how unfair and unreliable the state's court system had become. He revealed that thirty-three Illinois death row inmates received representation by attorneys later disbarred or suspended from practicing law. Thirty-five were African Americans convicted or condemned by all-white juries. In fact, more than two-thirds of the state's death row inmates were African Americans. Additionally, testimony from jailhouse informants was enough to convict forty-six of the inmates.[14]

Ryan stressed the importance of his position. "To say it plainly," he said, "the Illinois capital punishment system is broken. It has taken innocent men to a hair's breadth escape from their unjust execution."

Ryan described the situation as insufferable, "nothing short of a catastrophic failure." He added, "Our capital system is haunted by the demon of error, error in determining guilt, and error in determining who among the guilty deserves to die."

And he described his actions as the only resolution. "The legislature couldn't reform it. Lawmakers won't repeal it. But I will not stand for it. I must act."

Your employees want to align to legitimate values. Does management mean what it says, or is the mission statement just another page on the company Web site? To prove the values are real, you must explain why you think they are important.

How are your organization's values important? In what ways does management ignore them? What are the consequences when the organization fails to live up to its values? How is the current situation intolerable? What's the alternative to living up to the values and why is it unacceptable?

## Disparage the Vision's Opponents

To add emotional energy when describing your vision, you can point out the conflicting behaviors of your competitors, critics, or adversaries. Typecasting your opponents as lacking those values your organization deems important helps underscore your vision's significance, creates passion and competition, and fosters commitment.

When announcing the commuting of all Illinois death sentences, Ryan addressed his action's critics. "I realize it will draw ridicule, scorn and anger from many who oppose this decision. They will say I am usurping the decisions of judges and juries and state legislators." He expected criticism from prosecutors. "But prosecutors in Illinois have the ultimate commutation power, a power that is exercised every day. They decide who will be subject to the death penalty, who will get a plea deal or even who may get a complete pass on prosecution. By what objective standards do they make these decisions? We do not know, they are not public."[15]

In his first week at Alcoa, O'Neill refused an invitation to join a Pittsburgh country club because it lacked an open membership policy. The club required a company's CEO to belong in order to allow other employees as members; by demonstrating his convictions and refusing to join, O'Neill annulled the memberships of several other Alcoa executives. When he promised to enact a policy prohibiting Alcoa from paying for employee memberships to clubs with restricted admissions, one executive faulted him for stirring up trouble in his first few days on the job. To emphasize his values, O'Neill belittled the criticism: "What excuse am I going to use six or twelve months from now? 'I've just discovered my principles?' 'They were on vacation or something when I first came?'"[16]

Disparaging your competitors' values helps you explain your organization's values by contrast. Is superior customer service your goal? *The store down the street is all about low prices, but we choose to focus on service.* Looking to improve quality? *Other manufacturers promise faster delivery, but we strive to deliver exceptional products.* Committed to integrity? *Some companies offer lip service, but we believe in maintaining the highest ethical standards.* Pointing out the differences between your organization's values and those of its competition highlights the importance you place on your values.

Who are your organization's primary rivals, detractors, or foes? What are the perceived values of your closest competitors, and how do they contrast with those of your organization? What stereotypes can you draw about their values?

Note that disparaging your competitors is effective for motivating employees; however, I advise against using this approach as a sales tool. Suggesting that potential customers buy from you because your competitors lack your values will probably offend your prospects.

## Forecast Success

Predicting the successful realization of your vision builds employee confidence in your leadership. Alluding to past triumphs helps to confirm the likelihood of this vision's success.

---

### The first step in assessing risk is judging the likelihood of success.

---

Remember, assessing our chances for success is instinctive to the risk taking process. The more successful we believe we will be, the more willing we are to take a risk. If you want employees to take a chance on your vision, you must convince them success is inevitable.

Ever hear a campaigning politician promise, *Vote for me, and there's a fifty-fifty chance I'll balance the budget?* If you did, you probably voted for the opposing candidate. You are more likely to hear, *I'll balance the budget in my first two years in office.* Politicians know you will support contenders who are confident of realizing the promises of their platforms.

It is the same when stumping on behalf of your vision. Visions involve change and, whenever change is imminent, employees wonder what they stand to lose. They expect assurances that you've considered any contingencies in your plan. In other words, this better work!

Does that mean you should make false guarantees? If you, like so many politicians, do, you will lose your constituents' support. If results are promising but far from certain, explain how you will determine success. *If we prevent even a single serious injury, then we will be successful.*

Politicians also recognize how pointing out their earlier accomplishments establishes confidence. *I balanced my city's budget, and I can balance our state budget, too.* Employees want to know they are following a competent leader. After all, who would have more luck enlisting you for their Antarctic expedition team, a first-time neophyte, or Ann Bancroft? Reminding employees about your past success builds trust in your vision.

How will you measure your vision's success? What analogies can you draw, between this and prior achievements, that will help inspire confidence in your vision?

## Select Emotional Language

The right language is critical to creating an emotional impact. Symbolic words enhance your vision's meaning. Metaphors and analogies help clarify your vision while stimulating your listener's imagination. Repetition adds a mesmerizing rhythm to the message, making it unforgettable. Choosing effective rhetorical techniques makes your vision both meaningful and memorable.

### Chose Your Words Carefully

Many retailers offer good service, but Sears' management envisioned their stores as "a compelling place to shop." Russell Baker referred to the "patience of the crowd" at the March on Washington for Jobs and Freedom, while Martin Luther King, Jr., said the marchers stood in "majestic dignity." The Illinois capital punishment system had dangerous flaws, but George Ryan colorfully alleged that it took "innocent men to a hair's breadth escape from their unjust execution." Those subtle language differences are like using a megaphone when you speak: they add punch to your message, and help your voice to be heard above all the others.

## The English language is unique in its seemingly limitless supply of synonyms.

Where many languages contain a single word for a specific meaning, dozens of English words convey identical or similar connotations. If your vision calls for doing excellent work, try typing the word *excellent* into your online thesaurus and you will find more than a hundred alternatives. Here are just a few: accomplished, brilliant, commendable, crackerjack, cutting edge, dazzling, distinctive, exceptional, exemplary, extraordinary, faultless, first-class, first-rate, flawless, good, great, impeccable, incomparable, magnificent, marvelous, matchless, mind-blowing, notable, outstanding, peerless, praiseworthy, premium, priceless, rare, reputable, sensational, smashing, spectacular, splendid, sterling, superb, superior, superlative, supreme, top-notch, trustworthy, unblemished, uncommon, unconventional, unparalleled, and wonderful. Although close in meaning, each word implies something slightly different.

The variations in the meaning of those terms might seem immaterial, but the right words influence how you connect with your listener's emotions. For example, the word *home* provokes thoughts of family, security, and attachment, whereas *residence* seems matter-of-fact and unsentimental. Now consider the different implications between performing *flawless* work and creating *excellent* products, providing *impeccable* service, or offering *unconventional* advice. Like stories, the right language helps you speak to both the emotional and the intellectual sides of your listener's mind.

Colorful words stimulate your listener's imagination and—in return—make for a greater emotional bond. Addressing employees at the unveiling of a new company logo, UPS board chair and CEO Mike Eskew described customer service as a "wonderful tradition of serving our customers" and spoke of "the privilege to serve our customers." He recalled seeing employees providing service "with unwavering commitment...integrity...and reliability." And rather than referring to his audience simply as UPS employees, he declared them "the quiet heroes of American commerce."[17]

What's the difference between choosing expressive language and using jargon? Jargon is confusing—if you replace *error-free* with *seamless*, the message becomes ambiguous. Symbolic words clarify your meaning. When *highest quality* becomes *flawless work*, your meaning is unmistakable. In addition, flamboyant words add excitement and purpose to your vision. As an employee, what's more enticing: promising *satisfaction guaranteed* or pledging service that is *dazzling*, *mind-blowing*, and *unparalleled*? By selecting your words carefully, you will avoid the overused expressions that long ago devolved into jargon.

## Metaphors and Analogies

Metaphors are figures of speech with which we substitute one idea for another, and draw a parallel between the two for the sake of variety and to create a vivid image. Speaking to workers from UPS's New York City hub, Eskew referred to the 43$^{rd}$ Street facility as "the nerve center of American and global commerce."[18] Sears featured its "softer side." Ryan wondered why Illinois legislators "could not heed the rising voices of reform," and quoted Supreme Court Justice Harry Blackman who wrote "I no longer shall tinker with the machinery of death."[19]

We can use analogies to clarify understanding by relating one thing to another, or two different things to each other. Anyone who has ever taken a high school proficiency or college placement test is familiar with vocabulary analogies. *MONDAY is to TUESDAY as (a) DAY is to NIGHT; (b) JANUARY is to FEBRUARY; (c) TODAY is to TOMORROW; (d) CAT is to DOG. If you answered (b), you answered correctly.* But analogies are helpful for connecting new or hard-to-understand ideas to our listeners' emotional side, letting individuals relate concepts contextually to their existing knowledge. (The story of two stonemasons—"I'm building a great cathedral"—is analogous for having a vision.)

Winston Churchill strongly believed in using analogies. In an article titled "The Scaffolding of Rhetoric," which he wrote at age twenty-three, he said of analogies, "they are among the most formidable weapons of the rhetorician."[20] Urging a policy of war with Germany, Churchill told the House of Commons, "Death and sorrow will be the companions of our journey; hardship our garment, constancy and valour our only shield." On another occasion, he said, "Socialism is like a dream. Sooner or later you wake up to reality." Fittingly, Churchill's skill as a communicator prompted President Kennedy to analogize, in turn, that "He mobilized the English language and sent it into battle."[21]

In his "I Have a Dream" speech, Martin Luther King, Jr., adapted an analogy from the Bible, the Book of Amos 5:24,[22] when he proclaimed that those devoted to civil rights "will not be satisfied until justice rolls down like waters and righteousness like a mighty stream."[23]

Eskew related the reliability of UPS deliveries to consumer confidence: "In today's climate of uncertainty, when our neighbors and friends and customers see our brown package cars rolling down the streets of Manhattan...or small towns across the country...they take comfort in knowing that the daily rhythm of life...and commerce...moves on." Then he compared the former UPS logo—a 1960s design of a string-wrapped package sitting above the carrier's shield—to an old friend: "A trusted friend. A friend [who] has served us and our families well for over 40 years," adding "it's time for this old friend to retire with the grace and dignity it deserves."[24]

How can you employ metaphors and analogies to clarify your vision? If your vision calls for perseverance in the transition through major change, you could refer to that transformation as an object, rather than an event, or relate it to another process. But please, avoid the dead metaphors and deathly analogies of jargon—refrain from promising to *unlock the chains of stagnation* or proclaiming *change a two-way street.* Instead, get creative like the hardy Vonnie Bell and Mike Van Zile. Vonnie said staying in her stressful work environment was like reading a dreary book, but vowed to help write the story's ending. Mike's analogy linking bank processing troubles to the past quality issues of American car makers, and their subsequent loss of business to rivals Honda, Toyota, and Mazda, inspired his coworkers to join a problem resolution team.

What analogies and metaphors might clarify your vision?

## Avoid Tired Metaphors

Business language is full of old metaphors—called *dead metaphors*—now integrated into everyday use. Examples include *climbing the corporate ladder*, *hitting the glass ceiling*, and *reaching the pinnacle of your career.*

Business people are obsessed with lines. How else do you explain the countless references to lines in our business language?

Of course, we're all interested in the *bottom line*. We know that to increase profits, we need additional *top line* revenue, more production from all our *business lines*, and closer attention paid to each *line item*. We'd better move some of those expenses *below the line*. Otherwise, our forecasts will be way *off line* and we'll default on our *credit line*.

Some companies like to encourage *front line* employees to *color outside the lines*. Others take a *tough line* and want workers to *toe the line* while following the *Party line*. Regardless, you must *walk a fine line* lest you venture *out of line*.

Did you see someone *cross the line*? Go *online* to our ethics *chat line;* simply type "embezzler" in the *command line*. If you'd rather talk *offline*, use the *800 line* to call our *ethics hotline*. We've also got an *ethics helpline*—it's the same people, but the name sounds friendlier, so you're more apt to report wrongdoing. But please, don't call *Dateline*.

Our new *product line* is *top-of-the-line*. We need to keep the *assembly line* running, so we can keep our *price line* high. I hope they complete labor negotiations by the *deadline* and avoid a *picket line*.

Companies like to use sports metaphors. We're at the *starting line* now, but we need to cross the *goal line*. We've sent in our best *line-up* because the game is *on the line* and they're our *last line of defense*.

Organizational charts can be confusing, what with all the lines. You might have a *straight line* to one boss and a *dotted line* to another. It's best to have the *inside line* and a *direct line* to the CEO. Are you *in line* for a promotion? If not, call the *job line* to see what's available.

If you're in the leadership *line of fire*, and you talk like this, you might be *putting your career on the line*. Although metaphors help listeners understand your message, dead metaphors are over-used and sound clichéd. Be original and create your own metaphors.

Send all of the above dead metaphors to the *end of the line*.

## Repetition

Speaking is more effective for reaching your listeners' emotions than writing. When you are confident or excited, for instance, listeners can hear it in your voice. On the other hand, written communication allows your audience to recall your exact message later. To help listeners remember what you say, use repetition.

> # There are several ways to repeat yourself without seeming like you are, uh, repeating yourself.

Parallels are contiguous clauses or phrases with equivalent meanings, usually within one sentence. King used synonymous parallels in his March on Washington speech, linking phrases like "the motels of the highways and the hotels of the cities" and "from every village and every hamlet, from every state and every city." He also used contrasting metaphors in parallel: "It came as a joyous daybreak to end the long night of their captivity" and "hew out of the mountain of despair a stone of hope."[25]

A related repetition method is chiasmus, a figure of speech in which you reverse the order of words in parallel clauses. In his inaugural speech, Kennedy said "And so, my fellow Americans, ask not what your country can do for you; ask what you can do for your country."[26] Churchill had a special fondness for chiasmus. In a 1953 speech to the House of Commons, he said, "Solvency is valueless without security, and security is impossible to achieve without solvency."[27]

Repeating a word or phrase at the beginning of consecutive clauses or sentences adds a memorable rhythm to your message. Churchill promised "We shall fight on the beaches, we shall fight on the landing grounds, we shall fight in the fields and in the streets, we shall fight in the hills."

Might all this repetition immunize your employees against your message? On the contrary, repetition is memorable and it serves to remind workers of the behavior you are trying to instill. I encouraged employees to take initiative by pledging repeatedly, "I'll always support the actions you take, but I'll never support you for not taking action." To ensure customer satisfaction, I regularly cautioned workers, "Never promise what you can't deliver, but always deliver what you promise." Rhetoric makes it easy for employees to remember your wishes.

Television marketers know their messages are more influential when consumers view an advertisement multiple times. If you want employees to buy your vision, rebroadcast it often.

## Bigger is Better

Good leaders are visionaries. Great leaders convince others to share their visions by expressing them in memorable and inspirational ways.

While a sophomore at Harvard in the late 1960s, Kent Keith wrote a guide for high school student leaders. The booklet included a challenge for student leaders to do the right thing at all times, even if doing so goes unnoticed or unappreciated. Spelled out in what he called "The Paradoxical Commandments of Leadership," the ten principles reflected Keith's awareness that doing what's right provides greater personal meaning than receiving glory for our actions.

Copies of the pamphlet, first published by Harvard Student Agencies and later by the National Association of Secondary School Principals, reached nearly 30,000 readers over the next several years. Keith went on to earn a B.A. at Harvard, become a Rhodes Scholar at Oxford, attend Waseda University in Tokyo, and earn a law degree at the University of Hawaii. He then worked as an attorney, a member of the Hawaii governor's cabinet, a high-tech park developer, a university president, and as a YMCA executive. Keith went nearly twenty-five years without hearing so much as a word about his Paradoxical Commandments.

In 1997, while attending a meeting of his Rotary Club, Keith was surprised to hear the invocator recite the Paradoxical Commandments in the form of a poem attributed to Mother Teresa. Intrigued, Keith located the poem's source in a book about the beloved humanitarian, and learned his commandments had hung on a wall in Mother Teresa's children's home in Calcutta. In the ensuing months, he encountered people from all walks of life following the commandments he had written almost thirty years earlier. (His book, *Anyway: The Paradoxical Commandments*, is for people wanting to learn more about the commandments and the philosophy behind them.)

My favorite of Keith's Paradoxical Commandments is the following: "The biggest men and women with the biggest ideas can be shot down by the smallest men and women with the smallest minds. Think big anyway."[28]

Values-based leaders have a vision and convince others to share it. But when you share your vision, there's a good chance you will encounter opposition from those resistant to change.

Keith writes, "Big men and women with big ideas are threatening to small men and women with small minds." Succumbing to discouragement, most business leaders refrain from cultivating visions. However, successful leaders follow Keith's advice: "If your big idea is shot down, simply pick it up, dust it off, and get moving again."

Employees want to believe they are important and useful, that they are contributing to their organization's success. Workers are attracted to visions with grand aspirations. Adds Keith, "People want to make a difference; people need a reason to hope, a goal to work toward. Small ideas don't bring out our best. Big ideas do."

So think big! Have a BIG Vision and convince others to share it.

# Chapter 7

## Applying the Six Vital Integrities

> *"Authority without wisdom is like a*
> *heavy axe without an edge, fitter to*
> *bruise than polish."*
> -Anne Bradstreet

Leadership can feel like a scary business. Because—let's face it—we often make it up as we go along.

In fact, it may take some time to realize that you really *are* a leader. Sure, there was that exciting day when you earned your first promotion to the level of management. But, after the initial thrill subsided, when did you experience your first uh-oh-the-buck-stops-here moment? Maybe it was while directing a successful project—or one where everything went wrong. Perhaps it was firing an employee for the very first time, or saving a direct report from making a career-ending mistake. Whenever it was, you had to face this unmistakable fact: work was never going to be the same for you—ever.

So having finally realized that you were a leader, when did you figure out that you needed leadership training? After all, you were just minding your own business, fulfilling your duties in accounting, production, or sales, when someone put you in charge. And now you're supposed to not only oversee all those employees, but also do your own work, meet department goals, keep your boss out of trouble, and—well, you get the point. The pay increase is nice, but a little information on how this leadership stuff works would be much appreciated, too.

But once you actually realized that you were a leader who needed guidance, when did you first accept the fact that you were really, truly on your own? Was it when you heard management's arguments against spending money on training? Look, the company wants to help you grow—you are, after all, one of their greatest assets and everything—but belts need tightening around here. Besides, they explain, aren't the people bossing *you* around doing just fine without any of those trendy new "soft" skills? If you have any questions, just ask for help from senior management—you know, the people doing such a great job "leading" you.

Unfortunately, for a majority of the organizations I talk to, leadership training is either a luxury or a threat. And so I hear them telling their new managers, "Sorry, spending money for a workshop—let alone freeing someone up for three days—is out of the question. Training funds are easy targets for cost-cutting measures because they're really not all that necessary, are they? But then, so are employees (which is why we're too shorthanded to send you for training)." Meanwhile, I can also hear them thinking, "What if our new managers come back from this workshop better equipped to lead than we are? They might start questioning our decisions, or even passing us by on their way up the corporate ladder."

In other words, you *are on your own* in this position, and sometimes you will just have to make it up as you go along. But, luckily enough, you do have the six Vital Integrities as your guide.

At the beginning of my workshops, I ask participants to identify the leadership dilemmas they face every day. We record those issues on a flipchart and, at the end, we revisit their challenges and discuss ways to use the Vital Integrities for handling each one.

Leaders have many common problems, so I typically hear similar issues in every workshop. And because you probably have the same challenges, too, I have listed and addressed the most frequently asked questions below.

## How Do You Encourage People to Take Initiative?

As you now know, there are several obstacles on the path of freely giving away your authority. And you are also, by now, aware that most employees want to contribute, show their creativity, and take some risks, but their instinctive self-protection mechanisms interfere. So it is your job to help them overcome those fears.

Start by letting your employees know that you want them to demonstrate initiative. Too many managers take for granted that their employees intuitively understand that expectation. Want your employees to tell you when they observe unethical behavior? Great, but do *they* know that?

An Ethics Resource Center study completed in 2003 found that when organizations broadcast their desires for employees to report misconduct—by publishing formal standards of conduct, holding ethics training, establishing ethics advice lines, and creating systems for anonymous reporting—employees are twice as likely to report the unethical activity they witness.[1] When Paul O'Neill gave Alcoa employees his home telephone number, he was making it known that he expected hourly workers to come forward if management failed to address safety issues. Only when employees *know* your expectations will they be able to *fulfill* them.

Next, help employees understand that failures are both inevitable and permissible. Employees who attribute their past failures to personal incompetence will be hesitant to show initiative in the future. And be sure to celebrate the failures of workers who venture outside their comfort zones. When they fall off their two-wheelers, pick them up, dust them off, wipe away any tears, and put them back on their bikes—with your promise to remain close behind as they try again.

Remember, too, that there are no Purple Hearts for employees whose managers encourage initiative but shoot them down when they show some. If you want previously wounded employees to take initiative, you must create a safe environment for their ongoing risk taking. Immunize your mavericks against the Semmelweis Reflex—your knee-jerk rejection of their new perspectives, provocative questions, or voiced concerns—by welcoming their input while at the same time disregarding those inner voices trying to defend you from criticism or threats to your judgment.

## It is easier to trust others when you can trust yourself.

Remember that empowering employees to take initiative is only your first responsibility in giving away your authority. You must also describe the objectives, follow up along the way, and ensure that all the needed resources are available. Listen carefully, not only with your ears, but also with your eyes, to determine whether employees need you to fill the role of an advisor, or the role of a sympathetic listener. But if you see someone in trouble, offer constructive feedback, rather than waiting for that employee to sound an alarm. Also, don't forget to support your employees by loudly announcing throughout the organization how you have delegated your authority, and demanding that co-workers at all levels respect the authority you've given your staff.

Finally, resist the urge to micromanage. Set high expectations for your employees and for yourself—have faith in your abilities to train and motivate others. Once you trust yourself, trusting your employees is easy.

But sometimes it's your boss who resists taking initiative. When you need a decision right now, and your boss remains firmly on the fence, be a risk seeker. Just as there are situations when you must question a superior's decision, there are occasions that require you to question the lack of one. And if that seems too risky, do a values-based assessment: ask yourself how taking this risk validates your faithfulness to the organization's values, and then let your answer guide you to either take or decline that risk.

One additional bonus: when employees observe your risk-taking behavior, they will be encouraged to take more initiative themselves.

## How Do You Get Your Employees to Follow the Rules?

As much as I detest the organizational tendency toward illogical or outdated policies, organizations do need rules in order to function optimally. Rules describe how your organization wants its employees to behave at work. But many rules are really just ancient vestiges (literally left over from the beginning of the industrial age) addressing everything from being on time to dressing appropriately. Other rules are responses to the latest corporate scandals, enacted to deal with new classes of misbehavior, like fabricating profits and insider trading. Fear of civil lawsuits prompts organizations to implement rules aimed at limiting their liability by, for example, mandating common sense in insisting that employees wear their safety goggles and leave their firearms at home. The problem is, such rules focus on the past, or more specifically, on preventing people from repeating someone else's bad behavior.

Because of their emphasis on control, traditional management theories center on making and imposing organizational rules. In other words, organizations expect workers to comply with their rules, and believe that a manager's role is simply to monitor and enforce employee obedience. And yet, regardless of how hard managers try, some people still abuse the rules. What's more, control merely postpones the inevitable breaking of rules. As Eliot Spitzer, the New York attorney general who launched groundbreaking investigations into wrongdoing within Wall Street investment houses, mutual fund managers, and the insurance industry, told *TIME* magazine in 2002, "The cases against Wall Street are like stopping someone speeding on a highway. The other cars slow down for a while, and then, after a certain number of miles, they speed up again. The question is, how many miles before they start speeding again?"[2]

---

## The real secret to persuading employees to follow rules lies in your organization's values, and in living by the values you profess.

---

Still, the question remains: why *do* some employees violate the rules? What it finally comes down to is how people differ in their opinions of right and wrong. Some think all actions are categorically right or wrong, regardless of the circumstances. *Lying is wrong, period!* Others believe that the consequences of their actions determine what's right or wrong. *Hurting someone's feel-*

*ings by telling the truth is worse than telling a lie to protect that person's feelings.* Most of us fall somewhere along the spectrum between the two extremes, leaning toward one or the other.

In her book, *The Art of Ethics,* Elizabeth McGrath discusses the stages people go through on the way to ethical maturity.[3] Our earliest memories of our personal ethical behavior involve obedience, she says. When we obeyed an adult, we were good boys and girls. When we disobeyed, we were bad. Therefore, we learned to view the world in we're-right-and-they're-wrong terms. As we mature ethically, we recognize that we are entitled to our own opinions about right and wrong. We learn to reject authority in favor of personal free will—whatever the cost—and to accept right and wrong as conditional. Once we experience the consequences of our independent decisions, we begin accepting responsibility for our behavior. We do this by thinking before we act, thus giving some much-needed forethought to our impulsive, or irresponsible, actions.

---

## Rules focus on the past—on preventing people from repeating someone else's bad behavior.

---

The reason some workers follow rules more closely than others is simple: everyone is at a different place in their ethical maturity journey. Those who follow every rule—and tattle on those who bend some—are still in the obedience stage. And some people never do, in fact, advance beyond the point of deferring to authority. Others are just now realizing that they have ethical choices and are beginning to test the limits of their freedom, like rebellious teenagers—or baby boomers experiencing a mid-life crisis. Still others have reached the point where they carefully consider the consequences of—and take responsibility for—their decisions.

So, as leaders, is it really our job to make employees obedient? Or should we pull them toward ethical maturity? Unfortunately, too many managers prefer obedience, reasoning that telling employees what is best for the company is easier than teaching workers how to recognize it for themselves. Micromanagers certainly prefer obedience to independent thought. So do dishonest leaders who use hierarchical rank as leverage for imposing unethical demands. Subordinates may know that what the boss is asking them to do is wrong, but still go along with it out of fear. *I was just following orders when I shredded those documents.*

Employees who advance beyond obedience to the stage of using their free will are those most apt to defy the rules. This is the biggest growth cycle in ethical development, and the most confusing. Employees at this stage will inevitably face differences of opinion and uncertainty, and may blame their confusion on their leaders. At this point, they can either move ahead in the ethical maturity process, or regress back to obedience. And you can make all the difference—in which choice they will make.

Here's how: in addition to your basic job of enforcing the rules, you need to show employees how to recognize the consequences of their behavior. Let's say the policy manual states that employees who are tardy six times in one year are subject to a written warning, in addition to further corrective action, up to and including termination. The rule is highly effective for your obedient employees who fear termination and arrive early every day. But your free will employees will push the edges of that organizational envelope, even after a warning. *What's the big deal about a few minutes?* Rather than quoting the rulebook, instead tell them what "the big deal" is by explaining the side effects of their tardiness. If the company's technical support telephone lines open at 8:00 a.m., for instance, and an employee arrives ten minutes late, some customers are left waiting on hold. If a worker is late when the production line starts, other employees have to cover multiple positions—sacrificing both quality and safety.

Although it may seem ineffective initially, you will be teaching employees the process for making their own ethical decisions. In fact, you should include this process in your company's rulebook itself. Experts say the most effective codes of conduct include multiple choice questions involving the very types of ethical dilemmas and ambiguities employees might encounter. Such dilemmas might be similar to the one below.

You are having lunch with a computer vendor who does business with the company. The vendor offers to pick up the check. What should you do?

a) accept the offer because you consumed less than $25 worth of food

b) pay for the vendor's lunch

c) decline the offer and pay for your own meal

d) suggest that you both sneak out without paying

The correct answer depends on your organization's policies. If you prohibit employees from accepting gifts of any kind from vendors, they should pay for their own meal.

Supplementing the rules by offering some alternatives to routinely following them, will remind employees that they have ethical choices, and can actually start them on the road to comparing their options.

People will always break the rules. But it's your job to coax your employees to ethical maturity. Once there, they might still break the rules, occasionally, but at least they will know how to use the company's values as their guiding conscience, rather than practicing blind obedience to authority.

## How Do You Get Employees to Respect Authority?

I must admit some confusion when addressing this issue. I suppose that's because there are so many meanings attributed to the word "authority." *The American Heritage Dictionary of the English Language* offers several definitions.[4] Accordingly, my response depends on the connotation of each, and so I've outline the various definitions along with my varying responses to them below.

> *Authority is the power to enforce laws and exact obedience,* is one connotation. My response: If you are looking for the power to rule and restrain people, become a drill instructor. That's the only job I know of where you can command and control people and still get respect. Of course, the reverence afforded a drill instructor is not really respect—it's merely fear.
>
> Managers who associate authority with power also equate fear with respect. You might find power in authority, but you will never earn respect with fear.
>
> *Authority is a person with the power to impose rules and demand obedience,* is yet another connotation. My response: Many people have this power. Bureaucrats embedded within the hierarchy creating rules that foster conformity and deference. Micromanagers projecting their low personal self-esteem onto their employees and mistrusting everyone. Highly negative managers bullying workers with name calling, humiliation, or mental and physical abuse. And managers subscribing to the practice of forced ranking. But the thing is, all these authoritarians

believe their positions or titles confer instant respect. In other words, they confuse authority with leadership.

What about the positive uses of authority? People who hold positions of authority have access to resources—human and otherwise—and the power to use them for managing day-to-day work. That power is beneficial for use with routine tasks where the problems that arise always have a procedural solution. For example, when a computer monitor malfunctions, someone in authority can requisition a replacement simply by signing a form.

Authoritarians, on the other hand, look for similarly simple resolutions in all situations, including those calling for adaptation. For example, when confronted with a valued employee's sudden punctuality problem, the authoritarian refers to the HR manual and applies the prescribed punishment.

But here's the all-important distinction between authority and leadership: although abiding by the bureaucratic protocol necessary to exchange a broken computer monitor, a leader will seek to understand what triggered an employee's tardiness problem *before* proceeding with a remedy. The sudden change in behavior could indicate job dissatisfaction, or it could coincide with a new daycare schedule. Unlike the strict authoritarian, the leader addresses the problem's underlying cause first, reserving the policy "prescription" as a last resort.

When you use your authority solely to force workers into compliance, employees feel threatened by that power and they naturally withhold their respect.

***Authority is an organization with administrative powers,*** is still another connotation. My response: Organizations inflict their power over employees in a variety of ways, both intentionally and unintentionally. In some companies, an inherited culture commands compliance. One of my former employer's work ethic, for instance, was the stuff of urban legends. When the company acquired the community bank where I worked, management wanted to make sure the integrated employees worked hard. So they immediately expounded upon a corporate tradition of working seven-to-seven, six days a week. Although the culture was indeed one of hard work and long hours, the seventy-two-hour-a-week saga proved to be pure folklore. Nevertheless, management continued to tell the fib, and a dozen years later, when I helped train employees at a newly acquired bank, the first question anxious workers asked me was whether we really worked a seven-to-seven schedule.

If your organization's leaders live by the values they profess—like the leaders of Timberland, Morrison & Foerster, Wegmans, and Starbucks—your employees will admire and respect the institution. But if the leaders misbehave, you will need to concoct your own fairy tale culture for employees to respect.

*Authority is an expert with the power to influence or persuade others, resulting from gained knowledge or experience,* is one more connotation. My response: Let me begin with a story. I once worked with a geek who was out of alignment. He was very bright and knew the systems inside and out. But he felt the company had wronged him. So he had progressed to the point of doing only what someone explicitly assigned. *Can I fix it? Sure, it'll take two minutes. But you'll have to fill out a work order!* As time went on, he leveraged his knack for avoiding work into power. Every time someone described a problem to him—regardless of the complexity or effort required in fixing it—he pondered a moment, as though a solution was forthcoming. Then he said, "Huh, that's weird," and turned and walked away. Talk about *power*.

The more geeks know about their crafts, the higher their standing is with other geeks. So tear up the org chart—titles are meaningless in geek land. The geek who knows the most earns the respect of all the other geeks in the organization.

But sometimes, it's the experts who are the hardest to persuade. They cling to professional prejudices and long-standing beliefs. After all, who is Semmelweis-the-shipping-clerk to tell us how to redesign our marketing brochures?

This is a paradox. We disrespect people who are experts in their fields—the geeks—because they act and speak in ways we find annoying. On the other hand, we disrespect novices who think outside their mainstream duties to suggest new products or improved procedures. *Huh, that's weird.*

If you want employees to respect your authority, you must show them that you recognize and respect what they do best. And you must also freely give away your authority by allowing employees to share even those ideas and concerns that fall outside of their areas of expertise.

Although all those connotations are valid definitions, you can see my confusion when managers ask how to get people to "respect authority." Do they want workers to fear authority, to fall into line when they bark instructions? Or maybe they expect employees to worship their titles, while forgoing personal dignity and self-esteem. Perhaps their companies romanticize their cultures and expect employees to pledge allegiance to fabled customs. And if they reserve respect for people who think and act alike, what good is their respect anyway?

Fortunately, there's one more connotation with the definition of this word.

> *Authority is confidence derived from experience,* the final connotation says. My response: One way to interpret this is that experienced leaders command authority by exuding confidence. We know leaders must be both confident and hardy. Otherwise—as when leaders respond to stress with cynicism, pessimism, or denial—employees will give their respect to someone else.
>
> But I take this connotation to mean the confidence employees have in their leaders, a confidence derived from experiencing their leaders as living by the values they profess. Employees are searching for leaders who *prove* their credibility in action, and when they observe you proving yours, they will know you are worthy of their trust.
>
> True authority stems from the trust employees place in you. So, the more trust your employees feel, the more respect they will reveal.

Now that you know the true definition of authority in all its connotations, you should have a better understanding of how to *give away* your authority. After all, if your authority stems from employees trusting in your leadership, giving away your authority is a similar process. And the best way to give away your authority is to trust those employees who have revealed their trustworthiness through their actions.

## How Do You Promote Teamwork?

I think the word "teamwork" must date back to the origins of workplace jargon. What a wonderful idea: employees cooperating with one another, placing the organization's goals before their individual interests. Why then, is it so difficult—in fact, damned near impossible—to persuade employees to work together? Because, regardless of the lip service we give to promoting teamwork, we discourage it at the same time by means of our actions. Here's a typical—and I do mean *typical*—scenario:

> "Welcome to the organization. We just need a few signatures. The first document you need to sign is our non-compete agreement, which prohibits you from working anywhere in this country for one year after resigning. We fully expect you'll want to stay here forever, but please sign this form waiving your right to sue us, if we abuse you too much. We're happy to have you—but only permanently—on our team.
>
> "And if it's all the same to you, we'll assign you to one of our micromanaging team leaders. You'll like the slower pace that comes from your boss's lack of trust and low expectations. Don't be alarmed if your teammates grow to distrust you or doubt your capability—that seems to happen a lot on this leader's team. If it gets too bad, feel free to withhold your best efforts, complain, treat colleagues discourteously, and show disrespect for the entire team. Everyone else does.
>
> "Before you know it, we'll promote you to player manager. Then you can go head-to-head with your team members, competing for clients and sales, and all those other things we know everyone aspires to, like job titles, money, and power. Just be careful about sharing informa-

tion with others. If you end up helping them look good, they'll probably get the promotion you want. Before you act, always ask yourself, *What's in it for me?*

"If you fail, we'll help you pack your things. Of course, you could try pinning the blame on another team member, instead. And, come to think of it, you really might want to practice sabotaging your coworkers: forced ranking time is just around the corner, and we're a little short on C players this year.

"And if you have any questions about the computer system, just call our support team. They're five states away and three hours behind. They help us maintain our open communications—that is, whenever we can get through to them.

"We're glad you're here. Enjoy the synergy!"

Remember, people do what you reward them to do. Yet most organizations forget to reward teamwork. Instead, they build winner-take-all compensation systems around the private interests of individual employees. *Sell the most, and win that terrific cruise.* Despite this obvious disparity, most leaders seem to have no clue as to why getting employees to work together is their toughest challenge.

## Teamwork: a unified force.

But what's worse is that there are many other organizational factors that cause resentment and create uncooperative cultures. Centralized or remote operational sites separate coworkers, close off communication, and lead to those familiar "us vs. them" confrontations. Forced ranking systems breed rivalries among coworkers, so employees learn to help one another less, and hinder one another more. Organizations with up-or-out career path philosophies require workers to become leaders if they want to earn more money or participate in decision making. Competition for limited leadership slots inevitably pits talented people against one another, regardless of their management aspirations.

The best approach for getting your employees to work together is to structure their rewards, the organizational culture, and your vision, all around teamwork. Whether you have a team of 250,000 marchers like Asa Philip Randolph, three dozen bicyclists like Billy Star, or one fellow explorer like Ann Bancroft, vision inspires teamwork. Starr said, "A unified force of people made whole by the belief in a single mission has the ability to improve the human condition." Without vision, your team will, figuratively speaking, stand around looking at each other, wondering what to do.

Perhaps you have limited control over your organization's reward systems and its culture. But whatever your level of influence, you do have a limitless command of your vision. Remember to have a vision that clearly promotes teamwork, and, as John F. Kennedy did ("...ask not what your country can do for you; ask what you can do for your country"), articulate it clearly to others.

## How Can You Control Rumors?

---

# Wonder: *Verb*. To be affected with surprise, curiosity, or doubt; to wait with uncertain expectation; to question or speculate.

---

When people wonder—when they wait with uncertain expectation—their questions and speculations inevitably turn to rumors. The 2004 Atlantic hurricane season was one of the most devastating on record, producing sixteen named storms and six major hurricanes. Between mid-August and late September, four hurricanes struck Florida in an unrelenting fashion. In their wake, the rumors were flying.

One rumor accused the government of stockpiling bodies awaiting burial, stacking them in refrigerated semi trailers. As hurricane Ivan approached, another rumor had fleeing residents hurrying to buy gas before the government imposed rationing limits. Rumor expert Gary Fine of Northwestern University told the Associated Press, "Natural disasters are a major incubator for rumors. In the midst of things, people are looking for any kind of information about what's going to happen next."[5]

People seek stability, even if it means inventing their own explanations when faced with confusing and ambiguous situations. Not surprisingly, workplace rumors start when we leave employees in the dark, thus forcing them to speculate.

Researchers describe three primary classes of rumors.[6] Pipe dreams forecast great things on the horizon. Also called wish-fulfillment rumors, these predictions convey the desires and hopes of the employees who spread them. *I hear the raises are bigger this year. Word is they're firing the boss we all dislike.*

Anxiety rumors express employee fears. Common in transitional times, anxiety rumors provide workers an avenue for sharing their concerns with others. *I understand the merger will result in massive layoffs.*

Bitterness triggers aggressive rumors—also known as wedge-drivers. The purpose is to discredit or demean an individual or the organization. *She only got that promotion because she's a woman.*

Whether inspired by hope, fear, or anger, rumors originate when employees perceive their expectations will go unmet. For instance, an individual counting on job security might spread a rumor about layoffs. But in reaching out to coworkers this way, employees are searching for reassurance, or to have their hidden suspicions confirmed.

The best way to prevent rumors is to do away with the confusion or fear that leaves employees wondering. And the best way to eliminate that misguided wondering is by proactively demonstrating your organization's values through the use of the six Vital Integrities.

## How Do You Hold Employees Accountable?

"Accountability" is a buzzword for the post-Enron era. What it really means is this is *your* responsibility, so we're blaming you if something goes wrong.

We want our employees to take responsibility for their actions, but by definition, the word "accountability" is threatening. It underscores that management expects you to account for your actions. Just look at its synonyms: answerability, burden, culpability, fault, guilt, incrimination, and liability. And you want people to welcome the idea of accountability?

By placing the emphasis on personal accountability, organizations have destroyed teamwork. The trend is to push accountability down to the smallest segment of the workplace population, all the way to individuals if possible. At the bank where I worked, we used to focus on teamwork. Back then, it was common for people from different departments—a branch manager and a lender, for instance—to join forces to win a new account. Whose department got credit was unimportant. We paid everybody fairly, so personal efforts benefited the organization as a whole.

But like most companies, we began looking for ways to measure performance. Knowing the division, department, and individual who contributed the most to our bottom line became an obsession. We added thousands of cost centers to the general ledger; in fact, every salesperson became a separate cost center.

We assigned every account, new and existing, to individual sales-people. Their job was to end every accounting period with more accounts than they started with, all with higher balances and bigger fees. A new bonus plan rewarded the best performers. Management published the results so everyone could see where they stood in the rankings.

That's when all thought of collaboration ended. Branch managers stopped referring clients for investment services, fearing that trust officers might steal their accounts. Cash management representatives were suddenly too busy servicing their own accounts to help lenders research customer problems. And before they teamed up to chase new business, colleagues had to agree on how to divide the spoils.

You might imagine that introducing financial incentives prompted this winner-take-all behavior. In fact, accountability—in the form of the published rankings—is really what set off that reaction. Hey, who can think of bonuses when we just missed third-quarter projections, and management is looking to dish out answerability, burden, culpability, fault, guilt, incrimination, and liability?

If duty compels you to incorporate the word accountability into your organization's jargon, pair it with adjectives that will create less-threatening phrases like "team accountability" or "two-sided accountability." Better yet, substitute words like collaboration, cooperation, and teamwork.

While trying to get employees to embrace accountability, be sure you set an example. Most managers regard accountability as one-sided: they hold workers responsible for results, but fail to provide the guidance and resources needed to accomplish the job. And some managers even think giving away their authority means passing the blame downward. But if you value accountability, the best way to prove it is by living the values you profess.

## How Do You Handle the Pressure of Leadership?

Being in charge can be stressful. As researchers Suzanne Kobasa and Salvatore Maddi found, psychologically hardy individuals have a realistic perception of stress, a strong commitment to their work, and a fondness for pressure. Accordingly, hardy people actively accept challenges and take risks. (The techniques discussed in the first chapter of this book are helpful for cultivating your hardiness quotient.)

Leadership requires a lot of time. That's why long hours come with the job. Some companies compound the workload by thrusting leaders into the multi-function role of a player manager. Eventually, even the hardiest people get tired in this role. You need to regulate your energy—in other words, pace yourself—in order to sustain the mental strength required to deal with the pressures that will inevitably arise.

---

# Even the hardiest
# leaders need energy.

---

Research indicates that we have natural performance cycles that allow us to perform at peak levels for one- to two-hour intervals.[7] Then we need a brief rest to recover our energy and concentration. These cycles—called ultradian rhythms—occur several times a day. Forcing ourselves to continue working through our low energy periods leads to mistakes, irritation, and fatigue. Then, when pressures increase, we are in the wrong mental state to respond effectively.

When you find yourself losing focus, go do something else for a while. Get out and talk to your employees, like those leaders who like to manage by "walking around." Or simply switch functions by setting aside the paperwork and returning some telephone calls. Breaks restore your energy, alertness, and tolerance for pressure.

## How Can You Avoid False Commitments?

Perhaps you've experienced this: You assign an employee the task of preparing a report. Then, before you know it, three weeks go by and you are still waiting for the information. Or maybe you asked your boss to consider you for a promotion, and two months have gone by since any mention of an upgrade. Living by the values you profess may mean honoring the commitments *you* make, but how do you make sure that your employees—and your boss—honor *their* commitments to you?

---

## Some people break commitments in the very act of making them.

---

The answer to that question lies in understanding how commitments are broken. We associate false commitments with someone failing to make good on a pledge. But a broken promise is only the culmination of a false commitment. In fact, carelessness in making commitments is what causes most commitment problems.

To avoid this type of frustration, make sure all parties understand the commitment that they are making. Do you need a report prepared? Or do you need a report prepared in time for next Monday's 1:00 p.m. staff meeting? Do you want the boss to decide whether to promote you *right now*? Or do you want her to consider you for promotion when the next opportunity arises? Wondering ensues when commitments are unclear. *I wonder what happened to that report I requested. I wonder if this report takes priority over my other duties.* Clarifying expectations ensures a two-sided commitment: your employee knows when the report is due, and you know how much time you have allocated for its completion.

Also, watch out for hallow commitments. Some people are uncomfortable saying no to anything, so they postpone their discomfort by offering halfhearted assurances. *Let me think about that promotion. I'll discuss the idea with my boss.* Others are afraid to appear incompetent, so they over-commit. *Sure, I'll have that report ready by Monday.* If challenged, they attribute their broken pledges to memory lapses, unavoidable delays, or a boss's interference. *I planned to grant your raise, but my boss put a freeze on all increases.* But because they actually have little intention of keeping their promises, they've already broken their commitments the moment they make them.

The commitments people make to you are only as good as the commitments you make to them. When you consider your commitments carefully, the trust you generate eliminates needless wondering and frees employees to spend their time doing good work.

## How Do You Improve Workplace Communication?

Leaders can overcome many of their business challenges by improving workplace communication. In a 2003 American Management Association survey, respondents indicated that the two greatest challenges facing businesses were recruiting, training, and retaining talented employees, and implementing profitable business strategies. But when only half of our workforce understands their organization's business goals, it's no wonder more than four out of five executives in the survey identified communication as the most important leadership skill.[8]

Imagine checking your voicemail messages and hearing the following company-wide broadcast:

"This is the corporate communications officer with some great news for all employees. Management has just announced that third quarter earnings per share were sixty cents, an increase of 11 percent over fifty-four cents per share for the same period last year. Third-quarter profits rose 35 percent. The company earned $73.8 million in the quarter; that's up from $66.4 million from a year ago. Excluding discontinued operations, we earned $59.1 million. Best of all, ROA was 1.75 percent and ROE was 21.6 percent. Management thanks you for your contribution to these results."

Messages like this appear in employee voicemail and e-mail boxes every day, as part of corporate communication programs (or what some marketing types call—get ready for the jargon!—"comms"). In their efforts to improve communication, companies feed employees the only information they know how to convey—their financial data. But does knowing that the corporation's faceless stockholders earned six cents more per share because you knocked yourself out meeting departmental goals inspire you to work even harder?

Try reframing the message to make it meaningful to all employees:

"I have interesting news for all employees, customers, and stockholders. Management has just announced that third quarter sales were higher than last year. That means more customers are choosing our products over our competitors. They obviously appreciate the superior quality you put into every item, and they value the outstanding customer service you provide every day. In addition, third-quarter profits rose 35 percent. Higher profits reflect your commitment to workplace safety. By keeping one another safe, you've eliminated costly accidents and increased productivity. And I'm happy to say we've accomplished these results while further reducing emissions into the environment. You should be proud of your achievements."

In truth, few employees understand the significance of terms like ROA (Return On Assets); maybe a handful know how to calculate it, and of that handful, one or two can imagine how their individual efforts might influence the stated figure. So why talk about ROA at all? Usually, it's because most leaders are at a loss for words, so they use numbers to fill that void.

But as Sears discovered, too much financial talk can cause employees to overestimate the company's profits, mistrust management, and fight change. Workers want to see the connection between *their* values and interests and the company's. They understand that the company needs to make a profit. But they want to know how that profit relates to such values as quality, customer service, helping workers stay safe, or protecting the environment.

Leaders must be able to communicate inspiring messages that promote the organization's values. Possessing the ability to communicate your vision separates you from the great majority of business leaders—all those bureaucrats who hide in the shadows, wishing they knew what to say, while relying on their media relations staffs to inspire the troops.

## In many organizations, workers learn to suppress unfavorable information to prevent upsetting senior management.

Another corporate communication problem is the rampant fear of telling superiors bad news. Back in my computer geek days, I was a project manager overseeing a small group of programmers. Every month, the information technology department's leadership team met with two high-ranking company executives to provide an update on all ongoing projects. For the project managers, the meetings were coveted opportunities to interact with a couple of honchos. But from the department head's perspective, the meetings held career-threatening potential: if one of us frontline supervisors let slip that a project was even slightly behind schedule, the senior managers might think he had lost control. Since the meetings were unavoidable, his only option was to tell us what to say.

Each month, just days before our appointment with the top brass, he held a dress rehearsal. The project managers recited the information we planned to report, and then the boss coached us with what to add or embellish, and what to delete or downplay. He showed us how to blame our holdups on other departments, software vendors, or the weather. We learned what we could safely say without damaging his career and, as a result, our own.

When you avoid bad news, or inflict the Semmelweis Reflex on those brave messengers who bring it to you, you encourage employees to remain silent. WorldCom board members who investigated the company's financial scandal found that employees who knew about wrongdoing were afraid to speak openly, because they feared losing their jobs or facing senior management's ridicule. Freely giving away your authority also means creating an environment that promotes risk taking and encourages straight talk.

And to improve the communication of "straight talk," you must master both listening and speaking. Be candid. Cut out all the euphemisms, ambiguous expressions, and big shot catchphrases, and simply say what you mean. Find an emotional connection with your listeners by telling relevant and memorable stories. Change your illusions about listening by understanding your listening roles, paying attention to nonverbal signals, showing speakers respect, and making time to listen. And above all, don't forget to share your vision by framing your messages around the values both you and your employees hold dear.

## How Do You Manage Multiple Generations?

The American workforce consists of employees from four generations: the silent or war generation, baby boomers, Generation X, and Generation Y. Each generation has common life experiences that influence their behavior. Employers must rethink how they lead workers to accommodate generational differences, use everyone's best talents, and inspire workers from every demographic group.

Leading a multigenerational workforce is easiest when all workers behave according to prescribed generational stereotypes. But cultures are constantly evolving, and characterizations used to describe a group today are soon outdated tomorrow. For example, would you portray the baby boomers in your organization as cynical, morally judgmental hippies, prone to risk taking and careless binges, with dirty hair and a profound disdain for their elders? Yet that's how many viewed that generation in the 1960s. Imagine what might happen if you tried to lead baby boomers while making those assumptions about them today. Nevertheless, understanding recent trends—as well as common generalizations—is a good place to begin.

Workers from the silent generation were born in the 1930s and 1940s; most are retired, or planning to retire soon. Baby boomers are assuming their roles as workforce elders. At a point in life when boomers are looking for greater balance, work is becoming exceedingly rigorous. Employees face demands to work longer hours, learn new technology, absorb the duties of laid-off coworkers, and meet increasingly unrealistic goals. Boomers be-lieve they must outwork their fresh-faced, computer-savvy coun-terparts or face losing their jobs to lower-paid youngsters. Whether someone pushed them off the corporate ladder, or they jumped, many have found meaning in second careers; jargon-using HR people call these individuals *parachutists*.

Many Generation X workers are used to being in charge be-cause they ran the household after school, until mom or dad came home from work. Consequently, they prefer working inde-pendently and they resist authority derived from seniority or job grade. In addition, titles and power hold little appeal for Gen Xers who define success in personal terms, like being a good spouse and raising happy, healthy children. And being less ambi-tious in the traditional corporate sense frees them to act fearlessly when challenging the status quo or bypassing the chain of command.

## Generalizations are good for describing groups, but you need to know what particular individuals value.

Generation Y came along just in time to witness what hap-pens to loyal workers when companies merge, restructure, relo-cate, automate, or move jobs overseas. Many watched as the companies to whom their mothers and fathers devoted their working lives simply eliminated their hard-working parents' jobs. Although they benefited financially from the long work hours and dual incomes of their parents, few expect any extended bene-fits from their own employers. As a result, Gen Yers are unwilling to pay their workplace dues to earn future rewards; they demand cash up front for everything they do, and are aggressive when seeking recognition or promotions. Raised in front of a computer screen, they expect to work on short-term projects—preferably cool ones—that they can see to completion.

Recognizing the best in your multigenerational workforce means taking time to understand what each person needs to succeed. You must know who prefers working independently, and who likes belonging to a team. Who favors close supervisor interaction, and who prefers the freedom of empowerment. Who's uncomfortable with computers, and who fancies exploring technology's cutting edge. This is one more good reason to "rehire" your employees every day—don't assume that everyone wants the same raises, titles, or power, and find out what *truly* inspires your employees.

In a 2004 survey conducted by the Society for Human Resource Management, one out of four human resource professionals reported witnessing intergenerational conflicts among workers.[9] Respondents indicated that older workers believe dedication means working long hours and, as a result, they think Gen Xers and Yers are shortchanging their employers in that regard. On the other hand, many younger employees blame older workers entrenched in high-level positions for a lack of advancement opportunities. Despite those generational tensions, SHRM found that workers from all age groups share common measurements regarding job satisfaction, including benefits—such as compensation and health insurance—and values, like safety and job security.

Although employees have generational interests, fears, and aspirations, they all prefer working for organizations that exhibit values which closely match their own. So while generational influences might drive what individual workers value, values-based leadership is the best way to guarantee alignment with all four generations.

Recognize the best in your employees, whatever their age. Find the career path that's appropriate for each person. Resist ranking people with different talents and levels of experience against one another. And "grow your own"—that is, hire and promote internal candidates from within—so your best and brightest employees will stay for a generation, and grow up in the organization.

## What about Employees Who Stop Performing?

A business-to-business sales manager described for me a frustrating situation with a veteran employee. After consistently achieving his quarterly sales targets for two years, this seasoned salesperson unexpectedly went into a slump, missing his goals several quarters in a row. His fellow salespeople were meeting their objectives, proof that business was obtainable. Apparently, he just quit trying, failing to follow up on leads or company-sponsored initiatives. What, wondered his manager, had caused this sudden drop in the man's formerly stellar performance?

---

## When workers stop working, ask yourself, "What changed?"

---

What causes a good employee to go bad? Some human resource professionals are quick to blame abrupt behavioral changes on drug or alcohol abuse—*Hey, we're paying all this money for the employee assistance program, we might as well refer somebody.* Many managers attribute performance slides to that employee's incompetence, and conclude that the worker simply lacks what it takes to meet increasing job demands. Some condemn the employee for slacking off or growing complacent. Other explanations include personal problems, burnout, or being an overall misfit. A manager's initial sympathy—*is everything okay at home?*—can turn to outright frustration in a hurry.

When things stop working, the first question any good diagnostician asks is, "What changed?" What happened to make this fellow lose his inspiration to sell?

As it turns out, a lot had changed. Over the prior eighteen months, the company initiated several new pricing strategies, only to reverse course each time. In one fiasco, the company implemented drastic price increases without notifying customers ahead of time. When a few customers balked, the company sent its salespeople into the field to defend the price hike. But after one affected government entity complained in the media, a messy public relations flap materialized and the company rolled back its prices. Management sent a humiliated sales force back out to repair the damage. A few months later, the company slashed prices in an attempt to drum up new business. Customers and salespeople were wondering what to expect next.

The slumping salesperson placed a high value on integrity. He attributed his prior sales successes to the trusting customer relationships he had formed over many years. He felt the unannounced price increase wiped out that trust. How could he continue selling the company's services when he was unable to negotiate prices in good faith? Every sale subjected a customer to the pricing whims of the company's leaders. Every sale put his personal integrity at risk.

When workers believe their values and those of their leaders are very different, a sense of betrayal overcomes them. Warning signs include a sudden lack of initiative, loss of passion, and falling production. Some leave, but others feel trapped and stay, while growing increasingly cynical, even to the point of openly criticizing the company and its leaders.

It makes sense to wonder why any of the company's salespeople continued to produce—surely, they cared about integrity, too. Turns out, most customers shrugged off the higher pricing as just another escalating expense of doing business, like jumps in liability insurance premiums and healthcare costs. Others had failed to notice the increase. And only one customer had waged war in the press, and that customer belonged to the struggling salesperson. Because few customers complained, most salespeople considered the increases justified.

In addition, hardier salespeople recognized the limited control they had in this situation. But while management dictated pricing decisions, each salesperson *could* actively influence how their customers responded. When the time came to defend the increases, instead of taking the heat, they explained those boundaries to their clients, and because most customers could understand the need to follow orders, the hardy salespeople felt far less stress.

Always happy to offer advice—solicited or otherwise—I enlightened the sales manager on the virtues of applying the Vital Integrities to help his valued employee. First, since senior management appeared unwilling to fall on its own sword, the sales manager would have to throw them on it metaphorically. I suggested he talk to the salesperson, recount the big cheeses' boneheaded decisions, and vilify their subsequent actions. While disparaging management's handling of the situation, he should simultaneously praise the salesperson's integrity. Acknowledging that the company's behavior conflicted with the salesperson's values would help this employee pinpoint his sense of betrayal.

Next, I recommended that the manager highlight recent sales results and emphasize that, by refusing to fulfill his obligations to the company, the salesperson was, unfortunately, compromising his own integrity. After making that point, he ought to teach the salesperson how to safeguard his integrity by disclosing uncertainty in his sales approach. Like the hardy souls who lay bare their limited control over management's ultimate directives, this salesperson should learn to explain pricing fluctuations up front. By telling him that he must improve his sales, while showing him an integrity-protecting method of selling, this manager would help his salesperson to get back on track.

Finally, I warned the sales manager to find ways of demonstrating to the salesperson that he is not alone in valuing integrity. I told him to be a maverick, to challenge senior management's future stupid decisions—not quietly or timidly, but in plain fist-pounding-foot-stomping view—even when hierarchical authority looms from above. This salesperson needs confirmation that his immediate supervisor values integrity, too. By challenging new affronts to that principle, the manager will demonstrate his conviction to integrity and his commitment to the organization's mission. And that's what matters most.

## How Do You Handle a Micromanaging Boss?

Giving away our authority is a personal challenge. It involves sharing influence, prestige, and applause, while forcing us to deal with our personal insecurities. It means trusting others—and that means taking risks. Our bosses are equally vulnerable to this challenge. Many of them resist giving away their authority because they are micromanagers.

Some bosses micromanage because they can—their positions give them power, and they think they are entitled to use it. They incessantly interrupt you, reschedule your priorities and deadlines, transfer their crises to you, and take credit for your ideas. They consume your time by conducting endless meetings and commissioning a stream of unnecessary reports.

Other micromanagers are afraid—they fear falling short in terms of their own performances. Their fears lead to stress, and stress causes them to believe the worst. *She won't get this done, and we'll miss the deadline. He'll screw this up and make me look bad, and I'll never get that promotion.* Fear and stress prevent micromanagers from trusting anyone except themselves. Consequently, they strive to establish complete control.

As long as you work for a micromanaging boss, you will struggle in your leadership role. Remember, micromanagers distrust their employees, and they broadcast their misgivings through their behavior. Your employees sense your boss's doubts and wonder whether you are worthy of *their* trust. If you are working for a micromanager, you must confront the problem.

Try to understand why your boss mistrusts you—specifically. In other words, find out whether your boss mistrusts everyone, or just you. Be a risk seeker and ask your boss the following:

> "Am I fulfilling your expectations as a leader? If not, please tell me how to improve. Because when you meddle in my actions, countermand my decisions, or outright do my job for me, I have to conclude that you distrust my judgment. You're probably unaware of how your behavior leads my employees to wonder if I have any real authority; that's why they often go around me to you. You've made me responsible for getting things done, but by constantly overriding my authority, you're making it impossible for me to succeed."

If your performance does need improving, this kind of candid conversation with your supervisor can help position you to grow as a leader. On the other hand, because people avoid giving the boss unpleasant information, drawing attention to micromanagement behavior could actually help your manager recognize a leadership weakness.

But some people micromanage consciously and deliberately. Like drill instructors who prohibit their charges from making eye contact with them, deliberate micromanagers try hard to intimidate. Challenging micromanagement behavior is the equivalent of staring into the eyes of a drill instructor. It says that you welcome constructive feedback and are eager to work hard toward improving, but that you are unwilling to endure unwarranted bullying and second-guessing.

If your micromanaging boss is unreceptive, or proves unable or unwilling to change, you should consider changing bosses. Unchecked, micromanagement limits your opportunities to grow. Your micromanager will continue to ignore you, abstain from teaching you new skills, withhold company news from you, exclude you from decision making, and selfishly hold back the most demanding assignments. Your employees might see you as weak or untrustworthy. You will expect less from yourself. Your performance will reflect your boss's low expectations. And, lo and behold, another self-fulfilling prophecy will come true.

If your core personal values include principles like trust, respect, and helping individuals grow, then living by the values you profess requires standing up to micromanagement.

# Epilogue

I sat down one day to process the paperwork for a valued employee who had recently given his two-week notice. Like most termination forms, this one included a multiple choice list to indicate why the person had resigned: higher salary, spouse transferring, returning to school, retiring, or poor health. I had to check "other," because the list lacked an option for this employee, who was resigning because he believed the company's values and his values were vastly different.

The form's final question stands out in my memory. The question asked whether, given the opportunity, I would rehire this individual. I had completed the form dozens of times during the two decades I worked for the company, but on this occasion, the question cried out to me from the page. *Would you rehire this person?*

What if I *had* rehired this employee? Suppose, a few months earlier, I had met with him and asked the typical recruitment questions: Why do you want to work here? What are your interests and goals? Where do you see yourself in five years? What do you think are your strengths? Imagine if, like a good recruiter, I had taken time to show him how he could realize his ambitions, hopes, and desires right here in our company? In other words, what if I had repeated the alignment process we used in hiring to reestablish the connection between his values and the organization's? Alas, I neglected to rehire him, and another company's recruiter persuaded him to seek his aspirations elsewhere.

We now know that, in today's business environment, values are of central concern. But when the phrase *corporate governance* replaces words like credibility, honesty, and integrity, how can we expect our employees to remain aligned to the organization? Today's leaders must demonstrate their organization's values—not just in the moment of truth, but continuously and proactively— in order to secure their employees' trust. You need to show those employees, who enlist and persist with your organization because they connect with its values, how to stay aligned with your mission. Show them, through your behavior, that those values are for real.

When you use the six Vital Integrities described in this book, you will acquire and preserve the leadership credibility you need to "rehire" your employees *every day*.

# Notes

## Introduction

1. Walker Information, "National workplace study indicates companies fail to build loyalty among vital employee assets; paying the price in turnover costs," news release, September 1, 2003.
2. Watson Wyatt Worldwide, "Workers' Attitudes Toward Leaders Rebounded Strongly Between 2002 and 2004, Watson Wyatt Survey Finds," news release, December 14, 2004.
3. Walker Information, "National workplace study," September 1, 2003.
4. Michael W. Horrigan, "Employment projections to 2012: concepts and context," *Monthly Labor Review* 127, no. 2 (2004): 3-4.
5. Bureau of Labor Statistics, "BLS Releases 2002-12 Employment Projections," news release, February 11, 2004.
6. Ibid.
7. Robert Levering and Milton Moskowitz, "The 100 Best Companies to Work For," *Fortune* 151, no. 2 (2005): 61-71.
8. John Sullivan, "Retention Strategy—Why Do People Stay In Their Jobs," http://www.drjohnsullivan.com/articles/1998/net47.htm.
9. Boyd Clarke and Ron Crossland, *The Leader's Voice: How your communication can inspire action and get results,* from the synopsis on the authors' Web site, http://www.bluepointleadership.com/tlv/.
10. James Floto, "Wally Pipp - A Life of Irony," *The Diamond Angle* (November 23, 2001), http://www.thediamondangle.com/archive/oct01/pipp.html.
11. Sullivan, "Retention Strategy."

## Chapter 1

1. Andrew S. Grove, *Only the Paranoid Survive: How To Exploit The Crisis Points That Challenge Every Company and Career* (New York: Currency, 1996), 144-145.
2. Robert B. Reich, "Your Job Is Change," *Fast Company* 39 (October 2000), http://fastcompany.com/magazine/39/jobischange.html.
3. Grove, *Only the Paranoid Survive,* 115.

4. Richard Lacayo and Amanda Ripley, "Persons of the Year," *TIME* 160, no. 27/1 (2002): 30-33.

5. Robert Turknett, Lyn Turknett, and Chris McCusker, "Going First and Being Followed: Leading with Knowledge and Integrity," *GoodBusiness* 3, no. 1 (2004), http://www.southerninstitute.org/Resources-GoodBusiness -Content(32).htm.

6. Michael Useem, *The Leadership Moment: Nine True Stories of Triumph and Disaster and Their Lessons for Us All* (New York: Three Rivers Press, 1999), 8.

7. Robert C. Doyle, *A Prisoner's Duty: Great Escapes in U.S. Military History* (Annapolis, MD: Naval Institute Press, 1997), 4-6, 8-10.

8. Fred Vogelstein, "Mighty Amazon," *Fortune* 147, no. 10 (2003): 60-67.

9. David Pottruck, *Clicks and Mortar: Passion Driven Growth in an Internet Driven World* (San Francisco: Jossey-Bass, 2001), 144-145.

10. Ricardo Semler, *The Seven-Day Weekend: Changing the Way Work Works* (n.p.:Portfolio, 2004), 1-20.

11. Salvatore R. Maddi, "The Story of *Hardiness*: Twenty Years of Theorizing, Research, and Practice," *Consulting Psychology Journal: Practice & Research* 54, no. 3 (2002): 173-185.

12. Jim Collins, *Good to Great: Why Some Companies Make the Leap...and Other's Don't* (New York: HarperBusiness, 2001), 83-87.

13. K. A. Wallace, Toni L. Bisconti, and C.S. Bergeman, "The Mediational Effect of Hardiness on Social Support and Optimal Outcomes in Later Life," *Basic & Applied Social Psychology* 23, no. 4 (2001): 267-279.

## Chapter 2

1. American Management Association, "Getting People to Collaborate at Work Is Top Leadership Challenge, American Management Association Survey Shows," news release, October 31, 2003.

2. Watson Wyatt Worldwide, "Effective Employee Communication Linked to Greater Shareholder Returns, Watson Wyatt Study Finds," news release, November 3, 2003.

3. Watson Wyatt Worldwide, "WorkUSA®2002—Weathering the Storm: A Study of Employee Attitudes and Opinions," http://www.watson wyatt.com/research/resrender.asp?id=W-557&page=1.

4. BBC News, "Jargon 'baffles' office workers," http://news.bbc.co.uk/1/hi /uk/643416.stm.

5. DuPont, "DuPont Updates Progress Toward USD 900 Million Cost Improvement; Announces Work Force Reduction As Part of Competitiveness Actions," news release, April 12, 2004.

6. University of California, San Diego, "UCSD Directory Abbreviations," http://blink.ucsd.edu/Blink/External/Topics/Policy/0,1162,668,00.html ?delivery=&coming_from=.

7. Franklin D. Roosevelt, press conference, December 17, 1940.

8. Richard McKeon, *The Basic Work of Aristotle* (New York: Random House, 1941), 594.
9. Julie Spencer, "Proxemically speaking—body language in interviews," brainbox.com.au (August, 28 2003), http://www.brainbox.com.au/brainbox/home.nsf/0/371053AFCA951286CA256D8F003AE335?open document.
10. Stephen C. Lundin, John Christensen, and Harry Paul, *Fish! Tales* (New York: Hyperion, 2002), 75.
11. David Whyte, "Re-establishing Conversations," Ethos Channel, http://www.ethoschannel.com/personalgrowth/d-whyte/3_d-whyte.html.
12. Roger Ailes, *You Are the Message* (New York: Currency, 1989), 19-25.

## Chapter 3

1. Citigroup, *Citigroup 2003 Annual Report*, 2.
2. Attorney General of the State of New York, *In the Matter of Citigroup Global Markets Inc. (formerly known as Salomon Smith Barney Inc.)*, Assurance of Discontinuance (April 21, 2003).
3. Ibid.
4. Nancy Gibbs, Melissa August, James Carney, John F. Dickerson, Rita Healy, Sean Scully, and Nathan Thornburgh, "Summer of Mistrust," *TIME* 160, no. 4 (2002): 16-20.
5. Michael S. Josephson and Wes Hanson, *The Power of Character: Prominent Americans Talk About Life, Family, Work, Values, and More* (New York: John Wiley and Sons, 1998), 218.
6. Dennis R. Beresford, Nicholas deB. Katzenbach, C.B. Rogers, Jr., *Report of Investigation by the Special Investigative Committee of the Board of Directors of WorldCom* (March 31, 2003), 21-22.
7. MCI, "MCI Guiding Principles," *Ethics and Business Conduct at MCI*, http://global.mci.com/about/governance/values/Ethics_Tr_Br_Web.pdf.
8. Ethics Resource Center, "Major Survey of America's Workers Finds Substantial Improvements in Ethics," news release, May 21, 2003.
9. Hewitt Associates LLC, "See No Evil," http://was4.hewitt.com/hewitt/resource/articleindex/talent/see_no_evil.htm.
10. Wharton School, "Why Smart People Do Unethical Things: What's Behind Another Year of Corporate Scandals," knowledge@wharton.com (January 14, 2004), http://knowledge.wharton.upenn.edu/index.cfm?fa=viewArticle&id=911.
11. Attorney General of the State of New York, *In the Matter of Citigroup Global Markets Inc.*
12. Watson Wyatt Worldwide, "Declining Levels of Employee Trust Are a Major Threat to Corporate Competitiveness, Watson Wyatt Study Finds," news release, July 25, 2002.

13. Walker Information, "The Walker Loyalty Report: Ethics in the Workplace, Topline Summary," September 2003, 3.
14. Starbucks, *Starbucks 2003 Corporate Social Responsibility Annual Report,* 27.
15. Ibid, 5.
16. Ibid., 4.
17. Peter Asmus, "Starbucks: A Model Global Corporate Citizen," *Business Ethics* 17, no. 4 (2003): 17.
18. Ibid.
19. Alan Deutschman, "Inside the Mind of Jeff Bezos," *Fast Company* 85 (August 2004): 52.
20. Maurice E. Schweitzer, Lisa Ordonez, and Bambi Douma, "Goal Setting As a Motivator of Unethical Behavior," *Academy of Management Journal* 47, no. 3 (2004): 422-432.
21. Wharton School, "Goal Setting and Cheating: Why They Often Go Together in the Workplace," knowledge@wharton.com (July 28, 2004), http://knowledge.wharton.upenn.edu/index.cfm?fa=viewArticle&id= 1017.

# Chapter 4

1. Ralph Nader, accepting the Green Party nomination for President of the United States, June 25, 2000. Nader 2000 Primary Committee, Inc., © 2000.
2. Gary Hamel, "Strategy as Revolution," *Harvard Business Review* 74, no. 4 (1996): 69-81.
3. Robert Rosenthal, "Covert Communication in Classrooms, Clinics, and Courtrooms," *Eye On Psi Chi* 3, no. 1 (1998): 18-22.
4. Ralph L. Rosnow and Robert Rosenthal, *Beginning Behavior Research: A Conceptual Primer,* 2nd ed. (Englewood Cliffs, NJ: Simon and Schuster, 1996), 85-86.
5. Kelly L. Zellars, Bennett J. Tepper, and Michelle K. Duffy, "Abusive Supervision and Subordinates' Organizational Citizenship Behavior," *Journal of Applied Psychology* 87, no. 6 (2002): 1068-1076.
6. Watson Wyatt Worldwide, "Growing Worker Confusion about Corporate Goals Complicates Recovery, Watson Wyatt WorkUSA® Study Finds," news release, September 9, 2002.
7. Ibid.
8. American Management Association, "Getting People to Collaborate at Work Is Top Leadership Challenge, American Management Association Survey Shows," news release, October 31, 2003.
9. Ibid.

10. Wikipedia, encyclopedia article about Ignaz Semmelweis, http://en .wikipedia.org/wiki/Ignaz_Semmelweis.
11. Wayne C. Burkan, *Wide Angle Vision: Beat Your Competition by Focusing on Fringe Competitors, Lost Customers, and Rogue Employees* (n.p.: John Wiley and Sons, 1996), 60.
12. Robert B. Reich, "Your Job Is Change," *Fast Company* 39 (October 2000), http://fastcompany.com/magazine/39/jobischange.html.
13. Philip Augar and Joy Palmer, *Player Manager: The Rise of Professionals Who Manage While They Work,* (New York: Thomson, 2003), 29-30.

## Chapter 5

1. Marcus Buckingham and Donald O. Clifton, *Now, Discover Your Strengths* (New York: Simon and Schuster, 2001), 5-6.
2. Ibid.
3. Jared Sandberg, "Clock Watching Could Signify a Lack of Career Challenges," *Wall Street Journal,* June 30, 2004.
4. Paul Glen, *Leading Geeks: How to Manage and Lead People Who Deliver Technology* (San Francisco: Josey-Bass, 2002), 11.
5. George Leonard, "The Journey to Mastery," *Noetic Sciences Review* 19 (Autumn 1991): 27-30.
6. John Bissell Carroll, *Human Cognitive Abilities: A Survey of Factor-Analytic Studies* (New York: Cambridge University Press, 1993), 675-676.
7. Leonard, "The Journey to Mastery," *Noetic Sciences Review.*
8. Ibid.
9. Loren Gary, "The Controversial Practice of Forced Ranking," *Harvard Management Review* 6, no. 10 (2001): 3-4.
10. John F. Welch, Jr., *Jack: Straight from the Gut* (New York: Warner Business Books, 2001), 157-162.
11. Ibid.
12. Meridith D. Ashby and Stephen A. Miles, *Leaders Talk Leadership: Top Executives Speak Their Minds* (New York: Oxford University Press, 2002), 177.
13. Andy Meisler, "Dead Man's Curve," *Workforce* 82, no.7 (2003): 44-49.
14. Laurence Johnston Peter, *The Peter Principle* (New York: Buccaneer Books, 1993), 25-27.
15. Ashby and Miles, *Leaders Talk Leadership,* 25.
16. Bradford D. Smart, *Topgrading: How Leading Companies Win* (Paramus, NJ: Prentice Hall, 1999), 85.

## Chapter 6

1. Anthony J. Rucci, Steven P. Kim, and Richard T. Quinn, "The Employee-Customer-Profit Chain at Sears," *Harvard Business Review* 76, no. 1 (1998): 82-97.

2. Watson Wyatt Worldwide, "Growing Worker Confusion about Corporate Goals," September 9, 2002.

3. Steven Kasher and Myrlie Evers-Williams, *The Civil Rights Movement: A Photographic History, 1954-68* (New York: Abbeville Press, 1996), 114-131.

4. Katherine Wroth, "Billy Starr: One for the Road," *AMC Outdoors* July/August 2003, http://www.outdoors.org/publications/outdoors/2003/2003-starr.cfm.

5. Pan-Massachusetts Challenge, "Walk in the Woods Leads to Nation's Most Successful Bike-a-Thon," http://www.pmc.org/about.asp?ArticleID=83.

6. Jimmy Fund, "The Boy Who Launched the Jimmy Fund," http://www.jimmyfund.org/abo/who/.

7. Billy Starr, letter to the editor, *Boston Globe,* August 5, 2004.

8. Sara Aase, "Amazing Ann," *Mpls. St. Paul Magazine* 31, no. 9 (2003): 240-245.

9. Ann Bancroft Foundation, "Ann Bancroft," http://www.annbancroftfoundation.org/profile.html.

10. Cheryl Dahle, "On Thin Ice," *Fast Company* 86 (September 2004): 79-80.

11. Martha Lagace, "Paul O'Neill: Values into Action," *HBS Working Knowledge,* November 4, 2002, http://hbswk.hbs.edu/pubitem.jhtml?id=3159&t=leadership.

12. Paul O'Neill, speech given in October 2002 at the Berg Center for Ethics and Leadership and the Katz Graduate School of Business, University of Pittsburg, http://www.pitt.edu/~bergcntr/ONeill.pdf.

13. Ibid.

14. George H. Ryan, speech given on January 11, 2003, at Northwestern University College of Law, http://www.stopcapitalpunishment.org/ryans_speech.html.

15. Ibid.

16. O'Neill, speech at the Berg Center for Ethics and Leadership, October 2002.

17. Michael L. Eskew, speech given on March 25, 2003, to UPS employees and guests at the company's New York City hub facility, http://www.pressroom.ups.com/execforum/speeches/speech/text/0,1403,477,00.html.

18. Ibid.

19. Ryan, speech at Northwestern University College of Law, January 11, 2003.

20. Winston Churchill, "The Scaffolding of Rhetoric," 1897, http://www-adm.pdx.edu/user/frinq/pluralst/churspek.htm.

21. Nick Wreden, "Language: Churchill's Key to Leadership," *Harvard Management Communication Letter,* June 2002.

22. Michael D. Coofan, *The New Oxford Annotated NRSV Bible with the Apocrypha,* 3rd ed. (New York: Oxford University Press, 2001), 1311.

23. Dr. Martin Luther King, Jr., speech given on August 28, 1963, at the March on Washington for Jobs and Freedom. Accepted as part of the Douglass Archives of American Public Address. Prepared by D. L. Oetting, http://douglassarchives.org/ihaveadream.txt.
24. Eskew, speech at UPS New York City hub facility, March 25, 2003.
25. King, speech at March on Washington, August 28, 1963.
26. John F. Kennedy, inaugural speech given January 20, 1961, http://www.jfklibrary.org/j012061.htm.
27. Wreden, "Language: Churchill's Key to Leadership," *Harvard Management Communication Letter.*
28. Kent M. Keith, *Anyway: The Paradoxical Commandments: Finding Personal Meaning in a Crazy World* (New York: G.P. Putnam's Sons, 2001), 63-73.

## Chapter 7

1. Ethics Resource Center, "Major Survey of America's Workers Finds Substantial Improvements in Ethics," news release, May 21, 2003.
2. Adi Ignatius, "Wall Street's Top Cop," *TIME* 160, no. 27/1 (2002), 64-71.
3. Elizabeth Z. McGrath, *The Art of Ethics: A Psychology of Ethical Beliefs* (Chicago: Loyola Press, 1994), 23-50.
4. *The American Heritage Dictionary of the English Language,* 4th ed. (Boston: Houghton Mifflin Company, 2000).
5. Mitch Stacy, "Rumor Mill Working Overtime after Florida Hurricanes," Associated Press, September 25, 2004.
6. Jitendra Mishra, "Managing the Grapevine," *Public Personnel Management* 19, no. 2 (1990): 213-228.
7. Hara Estroff Manano, "Biorhythms: Get in Step," *Psychology Today,* http://cms.psychologytoday.com/articles/pto-20040428-000001.html.
8. American Management Association, "Getting People to Collaborate at Work Is Top Leadership Challenge, American Management Association Survey Shows," news release, October 31, 2003.
9. Jennifer Schramm, "Age Groups Mostly in Accord," *HR Magazine* 49, no. 9 (2004): 208.

# Index

## green press
### INITIATIVE

# The **Leading from the Heart** Workshop®

The name says it all: *The Leading from the Heart Workshop*® teaches leaders at all levels how to lead with heartfelt principles. This three-day workshop provides a unique opportunity to explore values-based leadership with author George Brymer in an intimate, small group setting. George presents an in-depth understanding of his six Vital Integrities in a fun and encouraging, hands-on environment. By balancing information with experiential exercises that are both practical and memorable, George ensures that the lessons you learn will endure long after the workshop ends.

To attend an upcoming public presentation of *The Leading from the Heart Workshop,* or to schedule an internal workshop for your organization, contact George at george.brymer@allsquareinc.com, or visit our Web site at www.allsquareinc.com.